Twelve Essential Topics in Early Childhood

TWELVE ESSENTIAL TOPICS

in Early Childhood

A Year of Professional Development
for Staff Meetings

NANCY P. ALEXANDER

Redleaf Press®
www.redleafpress.org
800-423-8309

Published by Redleaf Press
10 Yorkton Court
St. Paul, MN 55117
www.redleafpress.org

First edition 2018
Cover design by Ryan Scheife, Mayfly Design
Cover illustration by iStock
Interior design by Percolator
Layout/composition by Wendy Holdman
Typeset in Abril Text, Enzo OT, and Skolar Sans
Printed in the United States of America
24 23 22 21 20 19 18 17   1 2 3 4 5 6 7 8

Library of Congress Cataloging-in-Publication Data

Names: Alexander, Nancy P., 1941– author.
Title: Twelve essential topics in early childhood : a year of professional development in
    staff meetings / Nancy P. Alexander.
Description: First Edition. | Saint Paul : Redleaf Press, 2018. | Includes bibliographical
    references.
Identifiers: LCCN 2017034727 (print) | LCCN 2017049850 (ebook) |
    ISBN 9781605546391 (ebook) | ISBN 9781605545523
Subjects: LCSH: Childhood development. | Career development. | BISAC: EDUCATION /
    Professional Development. | EDUCATION / Preschool & Kindergarten. | EDUCATION /
    Research.
Classification: LCC LB1140.2 (ebook) | LCC LB1140.2 .A455 2018 (print) | DDC 372.21—dc23
LC record available at https://lccn.loc.gov/2017034727

Printed on acid-free paper

This book is the result not only of my years of experience but also of the many mentors, colleagues, and others who have influenced and inspired the work that went into this book. To all of them, I thank you.

Contents

Introduction

As a professional in the early care and education field, you've likely learned that training materials that are practical and easy to use is extremely helpful in the fast-paced world of programs for young children. In this book, you will find such assistance in your endeavor to provide effective and ongoing professional development for your staff.

Intended Audience

This book is designed for early learning program administrators to provide professional development for their staff in one- or two-hour sessions. Optional activities are included in each chapter to expand the training for up to three hours. This book is also useful for professional development specialists such as child care resource and referral staff, early childhood faculty, trainers, or others who provide professional development or coaching for early childhood staff.

Contents

Following general information on professional development best practices, adult education, and coaching, this book contains training plans on twelve topics common to early learning programs. Each chapter includes all materials needed to provide successful professional development sessions with a minimum amount of preparation.

Organization of Training Sessions

The sessions are designed to be flexible for the facilitator depending on the amount of time available and depth of training to be provided. The first part of each topic is intended to be conducted as a one-hour session. The second part may be added to provide two hours of training at the same time or later as a follow-up to the first session. Thus, the training plan can work for a center director to conduct one or two staff meetings of an hour each, or for group trainings as a two-hour session. Note, however, that the second part of each topic is not designed to be used alone since it builds on the information in the first session. Additional activities are provided that can be added to expand to a third staff meeting or for a three-hour training session.

Technology

A CD-ROM containing a PowerPoint for each chapter is included for use during training sessions. Additionally, the slides from the PowerPoint may be printed as handouts for situations where technology is not available. The PowerPoints are not essential to the professional development sessions, but can serve to maintain participant interest and to supplement the training. The CD-ROM also includes all handouts and other printed material needed to present the training successfully.

PROJECTOR AND LAPTOP

If the PowerPoints are used, a projector and laptop or other projection source will be needed. A light-colored wall or screen also will be necessary.

CELL PHONES

In two chapters, participants are asked to locate information on their cell phones. Tablets or other technology may be used as well. Primarily, this activity involves using a search engine to locate information from the Internet.

Materials Needed

For each topic, there is a list of materials needed by the facilitator and a list of materials needed by the participants. Also provided is a list of equipment and supplies necessary for the session. In some instances, options are offered if specific equipment or supplies are not available.

Some sessions require materials that must be prepared ahead of time. These materials are listed under the heading "Make-Ahead Materials." Most of these materials will require commonly available office or teaching supplies.

Index card printouts are used in some activities. Instructions for preparing the index cards are included in the "Make-Ahead Materials" section. Copies of the index card-formatted handouts are available on the CD-ROM. The information on the index cards is included as a handout for the facilitator to reference during the activity or to use as a handout for participants. That handouts sheet can be printed on paper and cut apart if printing the index cards is not feasible.

FLIP CHARTS

In a few instances, flip charts must be prepared in advance. Chapter 1, "Training Tips," includes information on preparation and use of flip charts. In most cases, dry-erase boards or poster boards may be substituted. However, flip charts are preferred because of the size and number of pages.

HANDOUTS

Each topic contains handouts for attendees. In most cases, one copy of each handout will be needed for each person taking part in the session. In some instances, such as small group activities, only one handout per small group will be needed.

In many cases, the handouts are designed for learners to note additional information, enabling the participants to make the handouts more relevant to their work setting or the ages of children with whom they work. Thus, facilitators can individualize the session to better meet program needs. Thumbnails of handouts are shown in the agendas for reference. All handouts and reproducible forms are available on the CD-ROM. Handouts are identified by the chapter number and the order in which they are used.

Agenda

Each chapter contains an agenda that provides specific instructions for conducting the training activities and suggestions for the amount of time to spend on each part of the training. Individual activities may need more or less time depending on the experiences of the participants, size of the group, or desire to address the topic in-depth. The recommended time should be considered a flexible guide.

ICEBREAKERS

In a few chapters, a specific icebreaker that introduces the topic is included. If an icebreaker is not specified, the facilitator may select an icebreaker from those included in chapter 1, "Training Tips."

PARTNER AND SMALL GROUP ACTIVITIES

Some activities are designed to promote discussion between partners or among participants in small groups. The agenda identifies when to select partners or divide into small groups. In a few instances, a strategy is given to divide the groups related to the content of the session. In most cases, any means of dividing participants may be chosen. If the activity is not identified as a partner or small group activity, then a whole group arrangement is assumed. Most activities can be adapted to alternative arrangements if desired.

ALTERNATE, ADDITIONAL, AND FOLLOW-UP ACTIVITIES

Each chapter includes alternate activities, providing for training flexibility. A trainer might choose to substitute one of the alternate activities to better meet program needs or their preferred training styles. Or these activities may be used in addition to the two-hour session if a longer session is preferred.

These extra activities may also be used by an administrator or a coach as follow-up to the training to support implementation of new skills. Such suggestions are particularly useful for program administrators working with their own staff to support ongoing program improvement.

Teacher Aids

In some sessions, material identified as teacher aids is provided to help the instructor prepare for leading a discussion or conducting an activity. The information is intended for the instructor's use, not as handouts.

Job Aids

Some materials are identified as job aids. Job aids are designed for a participant to take to their job site or classroom and post or use as a reminder of key information to support the implementation of new skills.

Resources

Resources for additional information on each topic are included for use by the facilitator or for participants for further study. Additional resources of a general nature are provided at the end of the book.

Evaluation

Check Your Knowledge questions are included to assess participants' mastery of the content. These questions are designed for use when both first and second hour sessions are completed. However, a trainer may use selected questions if only the first hour of training is conducted. Open-ended questions for each topic provide opportunities for participants to reflect on the training content. Although the assessment is designed to be submitted anonymously, the facilitator may choose to have names included in order to plan for follow-up activities with specific individuals. The format of this pre- and post-assessment makes it easy for the facilitator to quickly determine participant progress and additional needs or support.

Training Tips

What do you need to know to provide effective professional development? Are you a program administrator who wants to help your staff improve? This chapter provides many tips for both the beginner and very experienced trainer.

Training Design

An effective professional development session does not just happen. Good training results from the instructor's skill, knowledge, and ability to plan based on participants' needs. At its basic level, designing training requires finding out what participants need and want, selecting or creating appropriate activities to help participants learn what they need to know, and arranging the logistics of conducting training.

SETTING REALISTIC GOALS

A common mistake in training design is attempting to cover too much information in too short a time. Doing so sets one up for failure. Select the most important skills that participants need or the most urgent information they need to learn, and focus on those. Trying to cover too much content is the downfall of many training events.

Participants want to incorporate changes a little at a time. They need time to implement new strategies and receive feedback to feel a sense of mastery before going on to the next step. Cover a complex task in several sessions rather than attempt to include too much new information in a single session. Too much new information or new expectations at once can be overwhelming.

RELEVANCE

Participants often come to a professional development session with questions that they need answered or problems for which they want solutions. Consequently, participants must see the activities as useful to them now or in the near future.

How does the facilitator ensure that training is relevant? Needs assessments and surveys are a good beginning. Prior to the training, use a questionnaire to gather information about individuals' needs or observe them in the classroom to assess needs. Asking at the start of a session what participants want to learn will provide additional on-the-spot information.

Plan some open-ended experiences to allow attendees to participate in activities that relate to their work responsibilities. Giving participants actual case studies they are likely to experience in their own programs as discussion topics will help make the content relevant to each individual's needs. Use realistic examples as a basis for activities to increase relevance to participants' work.

PREPARATION

Preparation means having well-thought-out activities and materials that are relevant to the needs of the individuals attending. A good training event will appear to flow, with the facilitator moving the group through the activities in a smooth, seemingly effortless manner. Preparation means that the trainer

- ▶ knows what the participants need and want;
- ▶ has identified activities and experiences to address those needs;
- ▶ has planned a variety of activities that allow for interaction, a balance of experiences, and time for repetition and review;
- ▶ is thoroughly familiar with the activities and materials;
- ▶ has a plan for adapting activities and responding to unexpected needs or interests;
- ▶ has checked the room arrangement and taken care of housekeeping details;
- ▶ has checked audiovisual equipment to ensure proper operation;
- ▶ has enough handouts and supplies for the number of participants;
- ▶ is relaxed and ready to greet and interact with participants.

Guidelines for Planning

While there are many approaches to planning, some important factors include

- ▶ involving the various learning styles of adults, and
- ▶ having a balance of activities, such as whole group, small group, partner, and individual.

INVOLVING ALL LEARNING STYLES

Individuals learn easiest when information is presented in particular ways. Some will want to see what you are talking about, and some will prefer to hear the information. Others need to do the tasks. Ensuring that you include opportunities for each participant's learning style is essential to effective training. Here are some ways to meet the needs of learners who prefer one learning style to the others:

Visual learners Show them what you mean and give them something to look at. Use flip charts, posters, PowerPoint, props, and other visual materials to focus their attention. Use videos to help them see exactly what is meant and how to perform a task. Visual learners will want information in writing as handouts to take with them for later reference.

Auditory learners Some adults learn primarily through auditory channels. They will need to hear the instructor and others discuss ideas and situations. Include opportunities for them to listen to what others have to say. These folks will like small group activities and will want charts, forms, and procedures explained to them and discussed. Do not just give them information to read—they will want you to discuss, review, and explain printed material.

Kinesthetic learners Many adults need hands-on activities and will want opportunities to do tasks they need to learn. These learners will benefit most from supervised practice. Coaching participants while they do tasks will help them practice the skills they need to learn and feel successful. Kinesthetic learners will like role play, learning games, and hands-on activities. They will want to actually do art, music, and science activities, not just hear about the activities or see completed products. Remember that many tasks performed in early learning centers require enough practice to make the task a habit. Consider, for example, the steps in hand washing, cleaning and sanitizing tables, and, especially, diaper changing.

PROVIDING A BALANCE OF ACTIVITIES

Include a balance of whole group, small group, partner, and individual activities in your professional development sessions. Sitting still in a large group for long periods of time listening to someone talk will be tiring for most participants. Participants will often want to work alone, to work with others, to work with friends, and to have opportunities to meet new people.

Varying the types of activities between whole group, small group, partner, and individual helps hold participants' interest. It also facilitates interactions with a variety of people and the sharing of ideas. Forming small groups or partners helps address participants' physical need to move around. The moving around and change will create a sense of "something new happening" that rekindles focus on the topic.

Training Tools

Technology, flip charts, whiteboards, and posters are common training materials, but using them effectively requires skill. The following are tips for using common training tools.

TECHNOLOGY

Using technology such as PowerPoint can add much to training. However, having technology that does not function or is not ready for use when the session begins can be the downfall of an otherwise good training. Here are tips for using technology effectively:

▶ Arrive early to set up and test equipment. Participants arriving for a session with a presenter who is not ready starts off with a negative experience.

▶ Make sure you know how to use the equipment. If it is not yours, practice before the session.

▶ Consider the audience's view. Place the screen or arrange the chairs so everyone can see well.

▶ Check to see if you need to dim the lights and how to do so.

▶ Do not read the slides. The content of PowerPoint should be an outline and serve as a cue for discussion. The audience should be able to quickly read the text then listen to the trainer for explanations or elaboration.

▶ If you must add a lot of text to slides, as when you are demonstrating how to complete a form or report, provide it as a handout in addition to the slide. If it's too difficult for some people to see when you are showing them on the slide where to fill in information, they can refer to the handout.

▶ Avoid sitting with your back to the audience while showing PowerPoint slides. Use a remote to advance the slides so you can maintain eye contact with the participants.

FLIP CHARTS

There are two major uses for flip charts: to provide information to participants and to record information from participants. Flip charts may be prepared in advance to present information. They also may be used to record information and ideas from the participants in such activities as brainstorming or group discussions. In most cases, poster board or dry erase boards can be substituted for flip charts.

Flip Charts to Inform

Prepared flip charts are an effective way to communicate information to a group. Use these guidelines to make informative flip charts:

▶ Keep sentences short.

▶ Use bullets or numbers to help clarify content.

▶ Use illustrations or graphics as appropriate.

▶ Make letters large enough to be seen from the distance in which it will be viewed. Usually, letters need to be about 1½ inches high. Leave about 2 inches between lines of text.

▶ Do not try to put too much on a page. Think of a flip chart as a billboard. The message must be conveyed quickly and succinctly.

▶ If you make a mistake, cover it with a stick-on label or a piece of paper cut from an old chart and attached with rubber cement.

▶ Vary colors to help understanding. Use one color for major headings or key points and another color for explanations or examples.

▶ Use markers that do not bleed through, making the information on other pages difficult to read. Alternatively, leave a blank page between each page you use.

▶ Use the element of surprise. Uncovering a page attracts attention to the information. Keep information covered until it is needed to prevent participants from reading ahead and being distracted from current activities.

Flip Charts to Record Ideas and Suggestions

A more common use for flip charts is to record the suggestions or ideas of participants. When using flip charts for this purpose, the same guidelines apply. Here are a few additional suggestions:

▶ Write memory joggers lightly in pencil on the blank pages as reminders of key points that you want to make sure are included even if no one suggests them.

▶ Work from the side of the chart if you are the one writing. Turning your back on the group reduces contact.

▶ Paraphrase if you are recording key ideas. It is not necessary to use exact quotations.

▶ If you plan to refer to the suggestions later, place the pages on the walls around the room.

▶ For a permanent record of the information, copy to a small sheet of paper or take the sheets with you and enter the information into a computer file. Or take a photo of each chart.

DRY-ERASE BOARDS

Dry-erase boards, often called whiteboards, are available at most office supply stores in a variety of sizes. The boards make it possible for small groups to have a writing surface for their ideas and can be used in place of flip charts. Most of the tips for flip charts also apply to whiteboards. A whiteboard, however, must be erased to add more information. Here are tips for using whiteboards:

▶ If you want a record of the information on the board, have someone copy the information or take a photo of it before you reuse the board.

▶ Clean boards periodically with cleaner designed for that purpose.

▶ Keep permanent markers away from the boards to avoid accidentally using them on the whiteboard.

▶ Use a small easel to hold the board at the right height.

Room Arrangement and Its Effect on Training

Picture a large, community-wide planning event in which participants could choose to attend one of several concurrent sessions, according to their interests. In one session, the room was an appropriate size for the twenty people in it. Chairs were in a circle, and interaction was excellent. Individuals, eager to share their ideas, interrupted each other with suggestions and comments in rapid succession. The facilitator could barely write fast enough to keep up with the brisk pace of the group's ideas.

In another session, held in a large convention bay with chairs fixed auditorium style, the facilitator was having great difficulty getting comments or suggestions from the audience. The facilitator's lectern was set far back from the audience, creating an intimidating situation for participants. This distance, coupled with the sit-and-listen chair arrangement in the much too large room, stifled interactions from attendees. The difference in the two groups was the room size and the arrangement of chairs. The first room favored the exchange of ideas, the other inhibited interchange. This was an actual experience the author had that documents well the great effect room arrangement has on participation and interactions.

How do you select the room arrangement that is right for the training that you want to conduct? Here are some suggestions.

THE PHYSICAL ENVIRONMENT

Always check out the site ahead of time if you are not familiar with it. The key in room arrangement is to select an arrangement based on the plan for the training. Selecting the arrangement most conducive to the main activities of the training will help ensure its success.

Auditorium Style

Auditorium style is popular because it allows for the most people in the space available. This setting works best when large numbers of people, such as fifty or more, need to receive information from a presenter. However, it is often a poor choice for most training. This arrangement places the instructor in the front and everyone else facing him or her. The message given to participants is that they are to listen passively to the instructor. Auditorium-style seating makes it difficult for good interactions to take place among participants. Even when interactions happen, they frequently become exchanges between participants and instructor rather than between participants.

Classroom Style

Classroom style is similar to auditorium style except that rectangular tables are used and participants sit at the tables facing the instructor. This type of setting usually works with twenty-five to forty-five people. The tables are an advantage when the training requires a lot of writing or if participants need individual work space. However, the arrangement still restricts interactions in much the same way as auditorium style does. One benefit of classroom style over auditorium style is that participants can move to face each other around the tables for small group or partner activities.

Horseshoe Arrangement

A horseshoe arrangement is often a good setup for a group of fewer than twenty people. If the group is larger, the sides of the horseshoe become too long to facilitate interaction, or the tables are too far apart for participants to talk easily with those on the other side. Participants should not be seated on the inside of the horseshoe since that puts their backs toward others and limits their ability to see the instructor and talk to the whole group.

Conference Seating

Conference seating, using round tables, effectively promotes participation in small groups. Conference seating can work with any size group, but very large groups may require assistants to circulate and keep groups on task. The only disadvantage to round tables is that whole group activities may be awkward since some participants will need to turn around to see when one person is talking to the whole group. Round tables take up more space and will require a larger room than might otherwise be needed. Round tables also may present a problem when using audiovisual aids, because not everyone may be able to see the projection screen.

Break-Out Rooms

When several small groups will be working on a project at the same time, nearby rooms to which they can move is a convenience. Break-out rooms simply need to be large enough to comfortably hold the small groups of the preferred size. Having access to separate rooms reduces a major problem when small group activities are conducted in one room—several people talking at once is distracting and makes communication in the groups difficult.

Too Large and Too Small Rooms

If the room for the training is too large, it may be difficult for some to hear or there may be a sense of "nobody showed up." It may be hard to provide a sense of togetherness and cooperative learning. When you must use a cavern of a room, try setting up at one end or in a corner.

If the room is too small, participants may feel crowded and may not be able to hear well when in small groups because of the noise from other groups. If you don't have access to a larger space or break-out rooms, try spreading into the hall or adapting small group activities to partner activities.

THE EMOTIONAL ENVIRONMENT

Just as the physical environment affects how individuals interact, the emotional climate will equally affect interactions. The facilitator is responsible for establishing much of the emotional climate of the training session. Here are some tips for a positive atmosphere.

Prepare Participants

Let participants know what to expect ahead of time. Knowing when the session will end, what credit will be given, and where to park and enter the building if an unfamiliar site will help them feel secure in what they will be facing. Participants often want to know ahead the arrangements for breaks or lunch and even what to wear.

Meeting and Greeting Participants

Arrive early enough to be set up, ready, and available to welcome participants when they arrive. Speaking to as many participants as possible and learning their names if you do not know them helps them feel welcome. Personal greetings convey a sense of being well organized and prepared. Conversing with participants allows you to find out a little about them and what they want from the session. These conversations can help you individualize and make training relevant.

Provide Norms

People come to training settings from diverse backgrounds. Some have had a lot of experience in training environments; some will have little or none. Let them know what is expected by addressing these items:

▶ Do you expect them to participate? How?

▶ Are they welcome to eat in the room?

▶ Will there be a break or do they leave at any time?

▶ Is it all right to ask questions? How and when?

Creating Respect and Trust

Participants must learn that you are sincere and that you are not only knowledgeable in your field, but you care about them as well. Sometimes personal anecdotes will help them see you as genuine. Let them know about your experiences that are similar to theirs. However, too many personal stories may turn participants off to your message. Show that you respect them and value their opinions by using active listening.

Protect Egos and Self-Concept

Let participants know that making mistakes is acceptable. Participants often fear making a mistake or being embarrassed by not knowing an answer. Here are some tips to let participants know it's all right to make an error or not know an answer:

▸ When you make a mistake, call attention to it in a lighthearted way.

▸ Let participants know you do not have all the answers but can help them locate information they need.

▸ Use face-saving techniques such as these to respond to incorrect answers:

  · "In some situations it might work, but . . ."

  · "You may not be aware of this new research that . . ."

  · "I thought so too until I learned . . ."

  · "Does anyone have another suggestion?"

▸ In any situation where participants are required to answer a question or provide a suggestion (such as in some of the small group activities), provide an option of asking the audience or asking for a volunteer to answer for them. Such options provide an "out" if a participant is self-conscious or unsure of a response.

Roles of the Training Facilitator

As the person guiding the session, the facilitator has many roles in the training and will be primarily responsible for its success. This section addresses the many roles the facilitator or trainer plays during most training activities.

PROVIDING INFORMATION

The facilitator must be knowledgeable in the topic under consideration to make appropriate comments and offer information as needed. If not, participants will resent being in the session. It is, however, acceptable for you to say, "I don't know" when asked a question you are not prepared to answer. Adding "Let me find out, and I'll get back to you about that" will allow you to maintain credibility. Then make sure you do so.

A good facilitator also knows when not to provide information. Not speaking up when one knows information that another asks is difficult. Sometimes, however, the group needs to develop insight rather than just hear an answer. Asking the right questions to get participants to figure out their own answers and final solutions is frequently more effective than giving answers. In short, a good facilitator knows when to speak up and when to keep quiet.

PROVIDING RESOURCES AND MATERIALS

The facilitator can offer materials and resources for further information. Additional resources are helpful for those participants who prefer to study a topic in-depth or those who need a broader knowledge base. Suggesting books and other resources where participants can get additional information is an important function of facilitators. Making sure that participants have understandable and necessary materials for the session is part of this role.

EXPANDING ON KNOWLEDGE: GUIDE AND GOAD

The facilitator must start with where the participants are and add to their skills and knowledge. It's important to help participants seek information that will be helpful to them as they become more experienced. The facilitator will continuously stimulate learners to question and evaluate their practices and will challenge them, to help them see the "big picture" of long-term goals.

OFFERING ENCOURAGEMENT

The successful trainer lets participants know that their comments and ideas are valued. Making an extra effort to involve individuals who may be reluctant to comment in a group helps participants see that their suggestions are important. Comments from everyone should be encouraged and accepted.

KEEPING THE GROUP FOCUSED

When adults get together and have a chance to talk to each other, there is a risk of their becoming sidetracked into personal conversation. There is also the risk of a group digressing from the most important aspect of the topic under discussion. The facilitator must tactfully intervene to keep them on task. Here are some helpful comments to prevent digressions:

"Our time is coming to an end, so let's move on to . . ."

"I know we all have a lot to talk about, but our task today is . . ."

"That is an interesting topic, but it is more than we can address today. Perhaps we can include it next time."

"I see that is a problem, but since it doesn't apply to everyone, can we discuss it right after this session?"

STAYING ON SCHEDULE

Participants usually do not like feeling rushed and generally dislike getting out of a session late. Keeping track of the time is important to provide a sense of completion without going past the announced ending time. A good facilitator will judge the time needed for each part of the planned activity and keep the group progressing toward a conclusion within the allotted time. As facilitator, you are a meeting manager. You will need to know when to let a discussion continue and when to call a halt. You must recognize when discussion is waning and it is time to build consensus or summarize and move to the next topic.

CLARIFYING

Sometimes a participant's comment or the information presented may not be clear to all. The facilitator can offer an example or additional information to ensure that everyone understands. You may restate the comments, ask for more information, or ask the speaker to give examples or elaborate when a suggestion is unclear.

SUMMARIZING

The facilitator will find it helpful to summarize information, not only at the end but also during the discussion and at various times throughout the session. Regular and frequent summaries will reinforce learning, help the group stay focused, and move toward conclusion.

Fundamentals of Training Sessions

Every session will have some common factors to address regardless of the topic. Opening with a strong beginning sets the stage for a productive session and makes a good first impression. Taking care of housekeeping details immediately will prevent interruptions later. Ending on a strong note will help participants leave with a positive memory.

Even routine matters such as distributing door prizes or closure activities can reinforce the content of the session. They can add humor or they can support networking. Many activities designed to facilitate transfer of learning to the job site make good closure activities.

WELCOMING PARTICIPANTS

People like predictability. Participants will want to know what is going to happen and when it will happen. Give participants an overview of the goals and objectives at the beginning of the session. Tell them what to expect and about how much time each portion of the session will take. Review the participation expectations and any guidelines for behavior. Spend time to remove anxiety or apprehensions. Welcome participants and express appreciation to them for attending. Thank anyone who has contributed to the setup, organization, or preparation of the session. Let participants know you are glad to be there and enjoy being with them.

Start on time. You establish credibility during the first few minutes. Do not undermine your efforts by not being prompt and ready. Even if there are latecomers, begin on time and let the latecomers ease into the room. For ongoing sessions, such as a weekly class or staff meeting, failing to start on time sets the stage for participants to come late to future sessions. Once they start coming late, it becomes difficult to start on time, because they are not there!

Plan to keep on schedule to the extent possible and let participants know you will. Participants will worry about other responsibilities if they perceive that the session will not finish on time. They may even worry about ending early if they use public transportation or have arrangements for someone to pick them up. Generally, finishing five to ten minutes early to allow for individual questions will leave a good impression with participants. It is better to schedule another session they will look forward to than to keep them well past the announced ending time.

HOUSEKEEPING DETAILS

At the beginning of a session, provide an overview of the schedule. If in an unfamiliar venue, take time to address questions that participants likely want to know but may not have asked, such as these:

▶ Where are the rest rooms, water fountains, or vending machines?

▶ When will there be a break?

▶ What about lunch or snacks?

▶ What time will the session end?

▶ What if someone must leave early?

▶ How do they get credit for the training?

▶ Where do personal items such as purses and coats go?

ICEBREAKERS

An icebreaker provides a transition into the training content and often allows participants to introduce themselves. Even if participants already know each other, a good icebreaker can also send a message that you value participation and want to know about the participants. Some icebreakers can give you information about what participants want or need from the session. They can also add humor. Here are a few icebreakers to consider.

Jelly Beans

Make a poster listing the colors and questions below. Before you show the poster, ask participants to each select one jelly bean. As they introduce themselves, have them answer the question beside the color of the jelly bean they selected. Questions can be created to relate to the training topic as well. If the group is large, conduct the icebreaker in small groups or as partners. Then, of course, they may eat the jelly beans.

Red	What is your favorite leisure activity?
Yellow	What play activity did you enjoy as a child?
Green	What was your favorite toy as a child?
Orange	What play activities did you enjoy with neighborhood children or relatives?
White	What is the favorite toy of the children in your classroom?
Black	What items that were not toys did you enjoy playing with when you were a child?

Scavenger Hunt

Give small groups a list of items, some that are rather common and some more difficult to find. Each group tries to find the items in their purses, wallets, or briefcases. The first group to find them all gets a small prize. Then participants introduce themselves.

Name Story

Read the book *Chrysanthemum* by Kevin Henkes to the group. Use the story to open a discussion about how participants got their names. Ask participants to introduce themselves and then tell how and why their parents selected their name.

Magic Wand

Pass around a magic wand with the instructions "If you could change anything about your program, what would it be?" Participants pass the wand around, introduce themselves, and tell what they would like to change with a wave of the magic wand. Purchase a wand or make one by attaching a star to a dowel. To relate the activity to a specific topic, ask participants to tell what they would change in relation to their ability to do some task. Make the task related to the training content, such as communicating effectively with parents, working with challenging children, or having more science activities.

ENDING THE SESSION

Do not just quit when you have finished the activities. Provide a logical ending so participants will know when the session is finished. Plan the ending carefully to leave a good impression and to serve as a transition activity. Ensure that you have a good conclusion by including some of the following components:

1. Summaries and review—What are the key points in the session? What did each person learn?

2. Planned implementation—How will the participants put into practice what they have learned? Where can they get more information and support? What do they do next? Will there be any follow-up?

3. Evaluations and certificates—How did they like the session, and what did they learn? How will you use the evaluation information? What type of record of their participation is kept?

4. Trainer follow-up—What are you going to do now? Are there unanswered questions you will respond to later? Will you schedule another session? Will you let them know about other training opportunities?

5. What now?—What do they do next? Should they enroll in another session? If so, what and when?

Certificates can be copied from the back of this book or printed from PDFs on the CD-ROM. The PDFs can be filled out electronically. Included are 1-hour and 2-hour certificates with the author's signature and 1-hour and 2-hour certificates with a blank line for the director to sign.

CLOSURE ACTIVITIES

Specific closure activities can provide a final positive experience. Closure activities can help secure friendships and connections among participants and bring the session to a logical conclusion. Closure activities can include humor and contribute to participants' remembering the training as a positive experience. The following are some examples of closure activities.

Group Hug

The Group Hug is best to use when participants know each other, such as those who work together or have been together in training for an extended period. Group Hug provides closure to the session and leaves everyone on a positive note.

To perform a Group Hug, first have participants form a large circle. Ask them to put their hands lightly on their neighbors' shoulders. Then ask them to take three steps forward to form a giant hug.

Hand Squeeze

When participants are seated in a circle, a good way to end a session is the Hand Squeeze. Join the circle and ask participants to hold hands. Squeeze the hand of the person on your right, who then squeezes the hand of the person on her right, and so on. Continue around the circle until the "squeeze" returns to you.

A variation is to let each person—as they squeeze the next person's hand—tell what they like about their work or what they are going to do differently related to the training.

If participants are not seated in a circle, have them stand, form a circle, and cross their arms before they take their neighbors' hands. If desired, the squeeze also can be sent around a second time in reverse.

Bye-Bye

Announce that since the session is over, you want to give everyone a chance to say good-bye. Ask them to turn to the right and wave good-bye to their neighbor. If everyone follows the instructions, most will be waving to the back of their neighbors. This "mistake" usually generates a good laugh. Waving "hello" the same way at the beginning of a session can set an example that mistakes are okay. Give these instructions, then laugh with the audience at the mistake you made.

One Small Step

Remind participants of the words of Neil Armstrong when he took the first step on the moon: "That's one small step for a man, one giant leap for mankind." Ask them to think about the small steps they can take to make a difference with children, then to think about all the small steps that together make a giant leap.

The Longest Journey

Reveal a banner or flip chart with the saying "The longest journey begins with the first step." Ask participants to take the first step as they leave the training to implement what they have learned.

Working with Small Groups and Partners

Varying the format of activities can help maintain focus and keep participants' interest from lagging. Small group and partner activities are popular formats for training activities.

SMALL GROUP ACTIVITIES

Since adult learners need to express themselves, small group experiences are excellent learning opportunities because they give learners more chances to talk. Some participants may be reluctant to speak in a large group and will be more at ease in a small group. Adults bring many experiences to the training, and small group activities make use of that experience. The small groups also provide a forum for participants to express other concerns and to be recognized for their knowledge.

Guidelines for Working with Small Group

▶ Give instructions orally before dividing the group. Provide written directions if the instructions are complex or if there is an activity to complete.

▶ Be clear about the time limits. State the time the group activity will end.

▶ Have a person to keep a record of the group's work. Use flip charts or small dry-erase boards if the information is to be shared.

▶ Move to each small group in turn until they settle into the task. Use the time to clarify and further explain the assignment and expectations.

▶ Continue to circulate among the groups to answer questions or add pertinent information to the discussion. Ask questions to keep the groups focused and be available as a resource for information.

▶ Give a notice when the group has about five minutes before the time is up so they can wrap up their discussions.

Dividing into Groups

Usually, it is desirable to encourage participants to meet new people to work in groups. Meeting others with similar interests is one of the benefits of a training session. Dividing into small groups also gives the instructor an opportunity to change the dynamics of the training and to vary the interactions. Of course, you can simply have the group count off according to the number of groups you want. However, some here are more interesting ways to divide into groups:

Birthdays Separate into the months of birthdays. For four groups, January, February, and March will be one group, April, May, and June will be another and so on. You can easily divide into three, four, or six groups by the number of months you assign to each group.

Playing cards Pass out playing cards, one to each participant. If you need two groups, separate by color; if you need four groups, divide by suits; if you need five groups, divide by suits and face cards.

Name tags Color code name tags and give them out randomly. Have everyone with the same color go to that assigned group.

Stickers Put a variety of stickers on name tags according to the number of groups desired. The stickers can be seasonal or tie in with the training topic.

Division by candy bar Place a bowl of small candy bars on each table and invite each attendee to take one. Have as many types of candy as the number of groups you want. For example, if you want six groups, put six different candy bars in the bowl. Ask participants to divide according to the candy chosen—all Snickers will be in one group, all Hershey's bars in another.

Group Leader Tasks

Each group will need a participant to act as group leader. When you choose group leaders, select those who can keep the discussion moving and streamline the reporting process. Effective group leaders will

- ▶ lead the activity according to the instructions;
- ▶ keep track of the time so that the activity is completed in the allowed time;
- ▶ help keep the group focused on the task;
- ▶ take notes, or have a recorder take notes, of ideas suggested or conclusions that the group reaches;
- ▶ speak for the small group before the whole group.

Ways to Select Group Leaders

There are a variety of ways to pick a group leader or spokesperson for each group. The following suggestions are also useful when there are no volunteers:

- ▶ On the count of three, everyone points to a group member they want to speak for the group. The one who gets the most "points" is the spokesperson.
- ▶ Ask for the total number of feet in participants' households including pets (a cat = 4, a bird = 2, people = 2 each). The highest number is the leader in the group.
- ▶ Find out who has the earliest or latest birthday during the year.
- ▶ Ask participants to write their middle names on a sheet of paper. The longest middle name is the leader.
- ▶ Choose the person who has worked in the same job or in the field the longest.
- ▶ Ask for each person's mother's first name. The first or last alphabetically becomes the leader.

Disadvantages and Cautions

▸ Sometimes the learning environment does not allow for easy movement into groups. Lecture auditoriums or rooms with fixed seating are difficult to use for small group activities.

▸ Trainers are sometimes concerned that misinformation may be shared. Small groups may be led by a volunteer or someone less experienced than the instructor. As a result, participants may state inappropriate or outmoded methods as being desirable, and the other participants may leave with wrong information.

▸ Problem participants may interfere with the group process and, consequently, the learning.

▸ It may be difficult to estimate accurately the time needed since the groups' experiences, interests, and level of involvement will vary.

▸ The groups may lose the focus of the activity and begin off-topic or personal discussions.

Dealing with These Concerns

Try to include someone knowledgeable in each small group. To do so, select the people you want and make sure they each get different items that will result in their being in a predetermined group. For example, if you are dividing using cards, make sure each person you view as a leader gets a different suit card. Often if anyone makes an inappropriate suggestion, another in the group will counteract it. If you circulate among the groups, you can suggest an alternative to an inappropriate suggestion. Later, you can give correct information at a time when it will not embarrass anyone. The following statements are helpful in reacting to incorrect information that may be given in a small group activity:

> "Many people once thought that too, but current research tells us that . . ."

> "Under some circumstances that might be so, but usually we find that . . ."

> "What are some alternative ways to . . .?"

> "Can anyone suggest another way to . . .?"

Circulate among the groups. Listen to the discussion in each group and offer comments or ask questions to stimulate ideas and keep the groups focused. Small group discussion time is not a signal for the trainer to take a break; the trainer is an important part of the activity. Offer summaries of what the group is discussing to help keep them focused. Monitor groups and intercede to deal with problems if the need arises. Ask open-ended questions to regain attention if they wander from the topic. You may even sit down for a short time in each group and offer comments as a participant.

Have a reporting period with the large group to summarize key points. Reporting time will give you another chance to address incorrect information and to clarify misunderstandings.

WORKING WITH PARTNERS

Individuals new to training or the early learning field may be more comfortable working with a partner rather than in a small group. Sometimes, especially in auditorium seating, working as partners is easier than trying to separate into small groups. Many of the techniques for dividing into small groups will also work in selecting partners. Here are a few unique techniques to choosing partners:

▶ Give everyone a ticket or stub, making sure that there will be a stub for each ticket holder. If you have an odd number of participants, allow for three people to work together. You can make tickets or purchase rolls at office supply stores.

▶ Make a set of cards with items that go together, such as a fork and spoon, cat and kitten, shoe and sock. Participants find the person with the card that goes with their card.

▶ Count off each participant, "One, two, one, two." Then have all the twos stand up and move to another location and find a partner.

CHAPTER 2

Follow-Up and Coaching

Successful improvement and implementation of new skills requires continued feedback, assistance, and support. If you are a program administrator working with your own staff to provide professional development, you can implement follow-up support through additional staff meetings, classroom visits, and feedback through coaching. If you are a trainer or instructor and available to make follow-up visits, phone calls, texts, or e-mails, then the information in this chapter will help you get the results you want.

Why Coaching?

Regardless of how excellent a training program may be, many individuals desire or need specific assistance in applying new skills in their own work setting. Thus on-site coaching, whether provided by an administrator, a trainer, or an outside specialist, plays an important role in program improvement. Here are some of the factors that make follow-up coaching an important support to implementing change. What do individuals indicate that they want from coaching? Most want opportunities to

- get answers to individual questions they have regarding their work;
- express their ideas in a supportive environment;
- find out about appropriate resources or references;
- complete assignments that result in progress they can see;
- receive reassurance they are performing correctly.

What individuals do not want from someone who is attempting to help them is

- pushing them to make changes for which they are not ready;
- confusing them with too many ideas or too much information at one time;
- creating a feeling they are doing things wrong.

What coaches can do is

► provide a framework for solving problems;

► help participants identify and clarify the tasks they want to address;

► assist participants in setting goals;

► break tasks into manageable steps;

► recognize and acknowledge effort and progress.

What Makes You a Coach?

As an administrator or trainer, you have an excellent opportunity to make the work you do more effective through follow-up support activities by assuming the role of coach.

ROLES OF THE COACH

The coach is a trainer who may take on one or more of the following roles. Listed under each are the follow-up activities you may perform in that role.

Role Model

► Model and demonstrate appropriate ways of working with children, thus influencing the participant's behavior, values, and standards of practice.

► Conduct activities to demonstrate the skills and techniques being addressed.

► Provide a model for professionalism and appropriate behavior and attitudes.

► Be a person others admire or want to emulate.

Planner

► Select, design, and plan the learning experience and the sequence of learning activities in collaboration with the participant.

► Respond to the participant's needs with additional suggestions and follow-up activities.

► Adapt plans based on the participant's needs and interests.

Instructor

► Guide the learning situation.

► Suggest, but do not prescribe, how the participant might solve a problem or improve a situation.

► Use open-ended questions to help the participant think through possible strategies and evaluate courses of action.

► Demonstrate how to perform tasks.

Facilitator

▶ Help the participant assess needs, set personal goals and timelines, and develop a plan of action to meet the goals.

▶ Respond to the participant's requests or interests; provide ongoing guidance and support as new strategies or procedures are implemented.

▶ Help the participant evaluate progress in meeting goals.

Resource Person

▶ Suggest books, supplies, websites, and other sources of information based on the needs and goals of the participant.

▶ Assist in determining appropriate uses of resources that support the participant's plans.

▶ Encourage the participant to approach others as resources and make use of community resources.

Co-learner

▶ Learn along with the participant, sharing ideas and experiences in a collaborative environment.

▶ Help the participant recognize that there is rarely only one way to perform a task. The challenge is to find or develop the way that works best for the children, the participant, and the program.

Confidence Builder

▶ Encourage the participant to tackle new challenges and to engage in growth-enhancing experiences.

▶ Invoke confidence in skills and abilities and a willingness to set new goals through activities that build on prior success.

Advocate

▶ Assist in removing barriers to the participant's progress.

▶ Facilitate environments to maximize learning opportunities.

▶ Help the participant understand how to appropriately suggest desired changes to administration.

Personal Reflection on Your Mentor Coaches

Are there any individuals who were particularly influential in your early years in the early childhood field? Who were some of the people who made a positive difference in your life? Answering the following questions will not only help you understand the value of being a coach, but also give you insight into how your mentees may see you:

- Why do you think they took a special interest in your success and helped you?
- What qualities did you have that made them spend time with you and encourage you?
- What was it that made each of them a great mentor?
- What might these experiences teach you about how to be a coach for others?
- What did you learn from these role models?
- How can you use this information in your own role as a coach?

Moving from Trainer to Coach

If you are taking on the coach role from being a trainer, you may need to develop some new skills since you will now be working with individuals at their work site rather than a large group from various settings. You will now be a facilitator of another's development rather than a presenter of information. Here are some changes that may be part of this transition process for you.

Focus of the Trainer	Focus of the Coach
Emphasis is on presenting and covering content	Focus is on how to facilitate motivation and individual mastery of skills
Organizes for one-time or short-term relationships	Develops a professional relationship with an individual learner
Views oneself as being responsible for what goes on in the training setting	Shares responsibility for the learning situation with the participant
Often begins and ends with a lecture or presentation approach	Uses questions from the participant and provides information to help the participant make decisions and apply strategies through personal experience

Focus of the Trainer	Focus of the Coach
Encourages the participant to accept a particular view of the subject matter (e.g., "The most important component of working with parents is regular communication.") and often cites research to document	Encourages the participant to develop own views of the subject matter (e.g., "Based on your experiences and reading, have you found any component of working with families to be more important than another?")
Approaches a training situation as "This is what I think you need to learn and this is how to do it."	Approaches a training situation as "What do you need or want to learn? How can I help you?"
Doesn't always involve the participant in planning or designing the course	Involves the participant in all aspects of the learning process

By focusing on the participant rather than the content, you view yourself, the participant, the subject matter, and the learning environment differently. Your role is to create an atmosphere where the participant makes selections about what to learn, how to learn, and how to implement new skills.

The Skills of the Coach: Many "Hats" to Wear

As do most of us, you play many roles in your work life: you are someone's employee, coworker, supervisor, friend, teacher. And now you are going to be someone's coach. We frequently assume these roles without question or carefully thinking about the full responsibilities.

Let's start with a familiar example: the role of boss or supervisor. Think about the individuals you have worked under, or reflect on your own experience as a supervisor, and answer the following questions:

▶ What are the "hats" supervisors wear in relation to their employees? For example, a boss is expected to see that others follow regulations and policies.

▶ What hats might you wear as a coach?

Listed below are a variety of hats adults wear when interacting with people. These are part of your role as a coach.

HELPING OTHERS SOLVE PROBLEMS

Think about a time you tried to help a friend with a problem he was having. Did your attempts turn out perfectly? Unlikely. Even with the best intentions we may fail at helping others solve their problems. Why is this so?

Who Owns the Problem?

When people bring problems to us, we frequently have a tendency to try to give them answers to solve their problems. We may ask a few questions and offer a solution we think will work, feeling like we have been a good friend, coworker, or supervisor by doing so.

The problem in this approach is that we may not be the best at solving another's problem. We may be encouraging dependency on our expertise rather than encouraging others in learning problem-solving skills. Those who have the problem are in the best position to solve it because they are closest to the situation, and they may already know what they need to do.

Why do others ask for our help solving a problem if they already know the answer? Sometimes they want to know that another person understands and is willing to listen without judging. Sometimes they want confirmation that the solution selected is viewed as correct by another person whom they respect.

LISTENING FOR UNDERSTANDING

Most of us know that when we listen to others, we express our interest by making eye contact, nodding, and saying things like "Uh huh," "Really," and "Wow!" This is an important step in listening, but it will not help others learn to solve their own problems. To help another person, we must listen for understanding.

An effective communication tool is active listening, a method of reflecting your understanding of what the other person is saying and feeling. For example, a teacher states that she is frustrated with certain children's behavior, has tried everything, and nothing seems to work. You might restate her comment by saying, "It sounds like you want some more ideas on how to manage children with challenging behavior. Would you like me to help you with that?" Active listening helps others feel understood and creates an opening to provide the help they need to solve the problem.

STAGES OF CHANGE

Coaches help and support individuals in making changes that improve their skills. People who try new practices often do so because they want to find better ways to do things. The motivation may be external, such as a new job requirement, or internal, such as a desire to achieve a new skill, like learning a computer program to communicate with family members. In many cases, administrators will see the need to change and be motivated to implement the changes much sooner than staff will. Employees often take longer to accept the need to change and to commit to improvement. Below are some of the steps in the progression of change for both managers and employees to help you as a coach understand the process and guide the progress of change:

Management Stages of Change

1. Recognizes the need for change

2. Seeks a better way to do things

3. Determines what should be changed and how

4. Forms a tentative plan for the proposed change

5. Predicts probable reactions of others to the change

6. Forms a timeline or deadline for making the change

7. Implements the change

Employee Stages of Change

1. Denies or ignores the proposed change

2. May respond with anger or resistance

3. Begins to understand the benefits or the need for the change.

4. Accepts and adapts to change

5. Becomes committed to the new environment

Here are some questions that will help you as you work with participants to implement changes. First, describe the situation that you would like to improve in a program by answering these questions:

▶ Who are the people who will most likely support the change?

▶ What resources do you need to make the change?

▶ What are some ways everyone involved can have input into the change?

Getting Started

Coaching is about change. Helping people do their jobs better involves changing old habits and creating new ones. It means learning new skills and developing new competencies. How do we go about getting started in making the changes happen? Here are seven steps toward implementing change:

1. Find out what learners need to make the change.

2. Involve administrators if you are not the administrator.

3. Be clear on what is to be accomplished and why it is necessary.

4. Communicate to learners and identify their responsibilities before, during, and after change.

5. Select activities based on objectives, jobs, tasks, and needs.

6. Consider variety in activities and materials to address various learning styles.

7. Plan for follow-up and ongoing support.

FIRST IMPRESSIONS

Making a good first impression in your coaching role is important to be viewed as a professional. What you do and do not do before and at the beginning of the first contact will affect your success and rapport. Consequently, it is important to establish a professional atmosphere at the very start. Here is how to make a good first impression in coaching:

▶ Plan with clear objectives and meaningful activities.

▶ Practice giving instructions, if you need to.

▶ Dress a bit more formally than you normally might if you lean toward casual attire.

▶ Arrive at the agreed-upon time. Too early and you interrupt. Too late and you create anxiety.

▶ Set a friendly tone. Greet the participant by name.

▶ If you plan to observe in the classroom, explain that you may be taking notes to help you remember things you want to discuss or questions you have.

▶ Make the participant feel comfortable with you as a person, but remain professional.

▶ Make productive use of the entire session. Keep focused on the task at hand and treat time as a precious commodity.

BUILDING RAPPORT

If you are not the administrator providing the coaching, you will need to build rapport with your participant. Here are the steps to take to build the rapport for successful coaching:

Introduce yourself Participants are interested in knowing about your background and experience. Your introduction can strengthen your credibility as a coach. Provide information on your experience as a means of making material more relevant to your participants.

Get to know your participants Find out why they are interested in having a coach and what they hope to gain from it. Ask about their goals for their careers, both short term and long term.

Ask open-ended questions As a coach, the more you show interest in them, the more likely participants will trust you and value your help. Asking about their views, the problems they experience, or reservations they have will help build rapport. Find interests that you have in common and talk about them.

Use silence When you ask a question, pause and wait for an answer. Pausing shows participants that you want to hear what they have to say. Then use effective listening skills to understand what they are saying.

Be enthusiastic Showing enthusiasm about the work with participants will make them feel respected and generate trust. This trust will make participants more receptive of your messages.

Be understanding Let the participants know that you understand what their jobs are like and the challenges they have. When you acknowledge or demonstrate that you understand, it does not have to mean that you agree; it just means you have heard them. Make statements that demonstrate your understanding of their situation and needs.

WRITTEN AGREEMENT

Consider working with the participant to develop a written agreement to clarify roles. A written agreement helps create commitment and dedication to the process, making it a priority for each partner. Here is a sample to help get you started:

By creating and signing this agreement we, _____ and

_____, are committing to do our best to honor these rules.

As we spend time together, we will both try to
- meet at least once per _____, for at least _____ (amount of time);
- pick meeting places that allow us to talk freely and in-depth;
- give at least twenty-four hours notice if we have to cancel or reschedule;
- come to our sessions prepared, having completed any assignments or gathered any resources;
- maintain confidentiality and respect privacy; and
- work on our common goals, which include:
- (List goals here.)

_____

_____

TIPS FOR SUCCESS

▶ Use an outcome-based approach for planning.

▶ In developing your agenda for a coaching session, think about what will be different or what will happen by the end of the session. Write that outcome at the top of your plan to keep your focus. Ensure that all the activities work to achieve that outcome.

▶ Ask and record what has worked well so far. Mark and document progress while continuing to move toward the goal.

▶ Use a visible "who-does-what-by-when" action plan. Record commitments throughout the session, and review and summarize the commitments at the session end. Be sure the action plan is in writing and use it to check progress at the next session.

Reinforcement and Review Activities

Changes in behavior and practices rarely happen overnight. Learning takes time, and regular review and reinforcement are vital parts of the learning process. The information and activities below are designed to be used one-on-one with an individual to make the activities relevant to an individual work setting. The activities can be used to review a training session or as coaching experiences.

The crucial element is that follow-up and onsite assistance must occur for training to be successful. Adults need reinforcement and review for new skills to become a habit and to feel comfortable with their new skills. Adults usually need help in relating new information they have learned to their unique situation and working environment.

Inspector or Evaluator

Many group training activities can be adapted to coaching situations. The activity below can be used in most situations to help you evaluate needs, make a plan for improvement, and mark progress in implementation of new skills.

Provide a checklist related to the needs of the participant. Ask the participant to pretend that she is an inspector and must assess her own classroom. Tell her that just as a licensing inspector must see evidence of a regulation, she is to check off an item only if she sees it. For example, if the checklist asks for a discipline policy to be posted, then she can check that item only if she sees it posted, not just because she knows that the center has a discipline policy. Remind the participant to be detailed and accurate in her evaluation. Then work with her as she checks off items on the list.

- If criteria from licensing are used, this activity will help a participant be more aware of the regulations that she is required to follow.
- If a rating scale such as the Early Childhood Environment Rating Scale is used, then having a participant take on the role of evaluator can help her better understand quality and what she can do to improve her classroom's rating.

Schedule time to review the participant's findings at the end of the activity and make a plan for improvement based on her inspection. The plan might be a simple list of tasks to be accomplished.

Making Learning Last

For the process of mastering new skills and learning to happen, there must be support from the administrator and follow-up over a period of time. If we want training or coaching to make an impact in the job environment, we must plan activities to do before, during, and after sessions to help make the learning stick.

BEFORE COACHING ACTIVITIES

- ▶ Create an individual, job-focused plan.
- ▶ Design training with specific job objectives, job tasks, and prerequisites in mind.
- ▶ Include a variety of learning tools and techniques.
- ▶ Make quick-reference-card job aids for appropriate tasks.
- ▶ Create forms to use in tracking progress.
- ▶ Be sure there is the support of any decision makers whose approval is needed for change.

DURING COACHING TASKS

▶ Incorporate on-the-job examples and supervised practice.

▶ Motivate learners throughout the process.

▶ Vary approaches to presenting material and information.

▶ Share your own examples.

▶ Use commitment statements.

AFTER COACHING ACTIVITIES

▶ Use e-mail, texting, or phone calls to support participant's implementation of new skills.

▶ Conduct follow-up interviews with administrators about progress.

▶ Provide print or electronic media information related to the topic to increase understanding or for further study.

▶ Determine areas that need additional attention.

KEY POINTS TO REMEMBER

▶ Effective coaching supports the implementing of new skills a little at a time.

▶ Scaffolding adult learning is an effective strategy for improvement.

▶ Participants need time to learn and understand a new process.

▶ Too much information at one time is likely to overwhelm a learner and cause frustration.

We Are All Alike
• We Are All Different •

Materials for Facilitator

- Document, Agenda
- Document, *Check Your Knowledge Answer Key*
- PowerPoint, We Are All Alike; We Are All Different

Materials for Participants

- Assessment, *Check Your Knowledge*

First Hour

- Handout, *Alike and Different Icebreaker*
- Handout, *Supporting Diversity in the Classroom*
- Handout, Certificate for Hour One

Second Hour

- Handout, *Diversity Planning Sheet for Books and Songs*
- Handout, *Diversity Activities*
- Handout, Certificate for Hour Two

Equipment and Supplies

- projector and laptop
- flip charts or poster boards and markers

For First Hour

- flip chart or poster prepared as described under "Make-Ahead Materials"
- art supplies representing various skin colors, such as construction paper, crayons, and markers
- cell phones

For Second Hour

- assortment of children's books and songs from diverse cultures (See list of suggested titles in resources on pages 43–44.)

For Additional Activities

- school supply catalogs
- scissors

Make-Ahead Materials

For First Hour

Prepare a flip chart or poster board with the following definition:

> Diversity: The ways we are different; the condition of having unique characteristics.

Keep the flip chart or poster board out of sight prior to the activity in which it is used.

We Are All Alike; We Are All Different Agenda

First Hour Session

5 minutes   Introduce the topic and then introduce yourself (if working with a group that does not know you).

If planning to conduct the second hour session in addition to the first, hand out the *Check Your Knowledge* sheet to participants and ask them to complete the left-hand side of the sheet. When they finish, ask them to set aside the sheet and not to refer to it until the end of the second session. Tell them that even if they realize that an answer is wrong as they take part in the training, they should not change their answer. This form is to evaluate what they learned in the training and will be anonymous.

3.1

10 minutes   Icebreaker: Distribute the handout *Alike and Different Icebreaker*. Ask participants to walk around the room, talk to others, and find a way they are like each person and a way they are different. Ask them to use the questions as a guide but to feel free to ask other questions if they want. They may use the handout for notes about what they learn about each other.

If the participants already know each other, this activity will help them learn about interests they have in common. If they do not know each other, have them introduce themselves. When the time is up, ask a few participants to share something they learned about another that they did not know prior to this activity. Discuss how we all have some experiences, traits, or interests in common but also some that are different. Point out that none of us are exactly alike, but we all have much in common.

3.2

5 minutes   Ask participants to write a one-sentence definition of diversity and what it means to them. When they finish, ask a few volunteers to read their definitions. Then ask for a show of hands if the participants' definitions included any of the following words or phrases:

varied	mixed
different	like or similar characteristics
individual	unlike characteristics
unusual	religions
race	not alike
ethnic group	minorities
ages	unique

Ask participants to quickly find a definition of diversity on their cell phones and share what they find and where they found it. Discuss the various definitions they found and then show the flip chart prepared with the following definition:

Diversity: The ways we are different; the condition of having unique characteristics.

Explain that although diversity may be defined many ways, as this activity demonstrated, the definition on the flip chart will be the definition for the purpose of this workshop to provide a common frame of reference.

5 minutes   Review the Objectives Part 1. Discuss with the group what they will learn in this session. Ask for specific questions that they want answered during the training.

Objectives Part 1

Define what we mean by diversity.

Discuss ways to make all children feel welcome.

Identify ways to support diversity in the classroom.

Using a show of hands, divide the class into small groups by the following similarities: Grew up in the same town where currently residing, in a small town, in a big city, on a farm, in the suburbs, lived in many places. If necessary, combine or split groups to have three to six people in each group.

15 minutes   Small Group Activity: Ask participants to brainstorm ways they can help children feel welcome and build self-esteem regardless of their differences. Ask each group to list the suggestions on their own flip chart or poster using the title Ways to Support Diversity. Allow time for a spokesperson to share with the whole group. Post the lists so participants can refer to them during the rest of the session.

10 minutes   Small Group Activity: Distribute the hand-out *Supporting Diversity in the Classroom*. Discuss the information on the handout and give examples. Ask participants to add ideas or suggestions from the earlier activity to the handout. If time permits, ask a spokes-person from each group to share with the whole group. Ask them to keep the handout as a reference for ideas to implement.

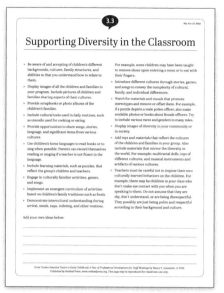

3.3

5 minutes   Show participants the art supplies that depict various skin tones. Point out how having these materials available recognizes the various skin tones of the children. Discuss how the availability of such materials conveys a message to children that the world consists of people whose skin colors are varied.

5 minutes   Review and summarize the content of the session.

Distribute certificates if presenting the one-hour session alone.

Second Hour Session

5 minutes   Review the Objectives Part 2. Discuss with the group what they will learn in this session. Ask for specific questions that they want answered during the training.

> ### Objectives Part 2
>
> Plan ways to use books and songs to support diversity in the classroom.
>
> Select activities to help children appreciate diversity.
>
> Review the goals of supporting diversity for children.

10 minutes   Show children's books that include children or families from various cultures or circumstances, calling attention to how they depict the culture. Explain how books can be used to help children learn to appreciate and value differences. Read one or two of the books, pointing out how children might identify with the charac-ters when the books show people similar to themselves. Sing or play several songs from other cultures appropriate for children. Discuss how the songs can show that diversity is respected and valued.

10 minutes   Ask participants to review the children's books to see how they depict diversity and increase self-esteem and cultural identity. Discuss how the stories help children accept and value differences. Tell participants you will make the books available following the session for them to peruse further. Ask each participant to select at least one book to use for the next activity.

Have each person select a partner. (See tips under "Working with Small Groups and Partners," on pages 20–23.)

15 minutes   Partner Activity: Have each pair review the books they've selected and the flip charts created in the first hour of training. Ask them to use the handout *Diversity Planning Sheet for Books and Songs* to make a plan for using one of the books and one of the songs (and the activities related to the book and song) to increase children's acceptance of differences. If time permits, ask volunteers to share their plans with the whole group.

3.4

15 minutes   Partner Activity: Distribute the handout *Diversity Activities* and review the suggestions on the flip charts from the first hour of this training for ways to support diversity. Ask participants to refer to the handout for ideas and to select at least three that they wish to conduct in their classrooms. Let each pair share with the whole group what activities they plan to incorporate into their curriculum. Ask them to relate their plan to the goal of helping each child feel welcome and valued.

3.5

5 minutes   Instruct participants to complete the *Check Your Knowledge* forms by answering the questions again and writing their new answers in the blanks on the right-hand side of the paper. Remind them not to change the answers they gave at the beginning of the session.

Collect the *Check Your Knowledge* sheets, then hand out certificates and any additional information or materials you wish to provide.

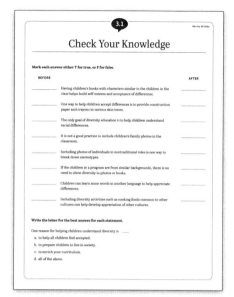

3.1

Alternate, Additional, and Follow-Up Activities

SELECTING MATERIALS AND SUPPLIES

In addition to the construction paper, crayons, and markers that depict various skin tones, provide school supply catalogs that show other art supplies and classroom materials. Have the participants look for toys and equipment that represent diversity. Ask them to make a list or cut out the pictures of items that they would like for their classroom.

WHO AM I?

Pass out the handout *Who Am I?* Ask participants to identify some unique characteristics or traits based on their cultures or family experiences. Ask them to think about a time they experienced an example of discrimination, prejudice, or intolerance and how they reacted. If desired, ask volunteers to share their experiences.

3.6

MORE CHILDREN'S BOOKS DEPICTING DIVERSE CHARACTERS

Expand on the Diversity Planning Sheet for Books and Songs activity in the agenda by showing additional children's books that depict diverse characters. Ask participants to review the books and decide how they might use the books to support children's understanding of differences. Ask them to use the books with children and to share their experience in a staff meeting.

Resources

CHILDREN'S BOOKS AND SONGS DEPICTING DIVERSITY

Books

- *A Letter to Amy* by Ezra Jack Keats
- *A Rainbow All Around Me* by Sandra Pinkley
- *Baby Rattlesnake* by Ata Te
- *Baby Says* by John Steptoe
- *Happy in Our Skin* by Fran Manushkin
- *It's Okay to Be Different* by Todd Parr
- *Love Is a Family* by Roma Downey
- *Margaret and Margarita/Margarita y Margaret* by Lynn Reiser
- *More More More, Said the Baby: Three Love Stories* by Vera B. Williams
- *One Afternoon* by Yumi Heo
- *Red: A Crayon's Story* by Michael Hall
- *Something Special for Me* by Vera B. Williams
- *Ten Little Fingers and Ten Little Toes* by Mem Fox
- *The Color of Us* by Karen Katz
- *The Sneetches* by Dr. Seuss
- *Tutus Aren't My Style* by Linda Skeers
- *We're Different, We're the Same* by Bobbi Kates
- *What a Wonderful World* by George David Weiss
- *Where Did You Get Your Moccasins?* by Bernelda Wheeler
- *Whistle for Willie* by Ezra Jack Keats
- *Why Am I Different?* by Norma Simon

Songs

- ▶ "All Time Favorite Dances" CD by Kimbo Educational

- ▶ "Best Multicultural Songs for Kids" CD by Kimbo Educational

- ▶ "Children of the World" CD by Kimbo Educational

- ▶ "Multicultural Bean Bag Fun" CD by Kimbo Educational

- ▶ "Multi-Cultural Children's Songs" by Ella Jenkins

- ▶ "Multicultural Lullabies around the World" CD by Sara Jordan

- ▶ "Multicultural Movement Fun" CD by Kimbo Educational

- ▶ "Putumayo Kids CD Collection," set of 7 CDs from Hatch Early Learning

Additional Resources

- ▶ NAEYC (National Association for the Education of Young Children). 1995. *Responding to Linguistic and Cultural Diversity: Recommendations for Effective Early Childhood Education.* https://www.naeyc.org/files/naeyc/file/positions/PSDIV98.PDF.

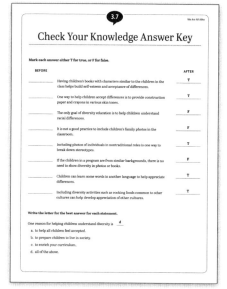

3.7

CHAPTER 4

Focusing on Families

Materials for Facilitator

- ▶ Document, Agenda
- ▶ Document, *Check Your Knowledge Answer Key*
- ▶ PowerPoint, Focusing on Families

Materials for Participants

- ▶ Assessment, *Check Your Knowledge*

First Hour

- ▶ Handout, *The Many Forms of Family Involvement*
- ▶ Handout, *How Will I Involve Families in My Classroom?*
- ▶ Handout, *Top Ten List of What Parents Want from Their Child's Program*
- ▶ Handout, Certificate for Hour One

Second Hour

- ▶ Handout, *Involving Fathers and Other Significant Male Figures*
- ▶ Handout, *Special Needs of Grandparents Raising Grandchildren*
- ▶ Handout, *The Needs of Teen and Very Young Parents*
- ▶ Handout, *Welcoming Parents Every Day*
- ▶ Handout, Certificate for Hour Two

Equipment and Supplies

- ▶ projector and laptop
- ▶ flip charts or poster boards and markers

For First Hour

- ▶ flip charts or posters for My Childhood Icebreaker as prepared under "Make-Ahead Materials"
- ▶ colored stickers

For Second Hour

- ▶ children's books depicting diverse families (See list of suggested titles in resources on page 53.)
- ▶ construction paper
- ▶ markers

Make-Ahead Materials

For First Hour

My Childhood Icebreaker: Prepare flip charts or posters with the titles Only Child, Youngest Child, Eldest Child, Lived in a Big City, Lived in a Small Town, Moved Several Times, Spent Much Time with Cousins and Relatives.

Focusing on Families Agenda

First Hour Session

5 minutes

Introduce the topic and then introduce yourself (if working with a group that does not know you).

If planning to conduct the second hour session in addition to the first, pass out the *Check Your Knowledge* sheet to participants and ask them to complete the left-hand side of the sheet. When they finish, ask them to set aside the sheet and not to refer to it until the end of the second session. Tell them that even if they realize that an answer is wrong as they take part in the training, they should not change their answer. This form is to evaluate what they learned in the training and will be anonymous.

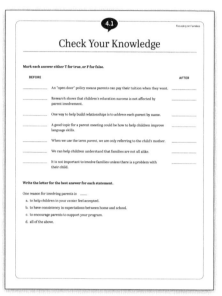

4.1

5 minutes

Icebreaker: My Childhood. Prior to participants' arrival, hang the My Childhood Icebreaker flip charts you prepared ahead of time. As the participants arrive, give each of them three colored stickers. Participants should place a sticker and write their names on each flip chart under the category that applies to them. If the group does not know each other, they should introduce themselves. If they know each other, the activity tells how their backgrounds are similar or different. Either way, the activity will provide information about common experiences. Point out how we are all affected by the families and circumstances in which we are raised.

5 minutes

Review the Objectives Part 1. Discuss with the group what they will learn in the session. Ask for specific questions that they want answered during the training.

Objectives Part 1

Describe why parents should be involved in their child's program.

Identify ways to get families involved.

Plan ways to involve parents in individual classrooms.

Emphasize that in this workshop when the term *parent* is used, it applies to the child's main caregiver and families. Point out that often grandparents and others function as the primary caregivers. Explain how parent involvement can mean anything we do to communicate with and include families in our program.

10 minutes   Give some examples of cooperative relations between caregiver and parents and some examples of how families have changed over time. Discuss how parents with children in the program can be the new extended family. Point out the importance of respecting parents of all cultures and backgrounds. Ask volunteers to share their own experiences and ideas of friendships and bonds between parents who met because their children attended the same program.

Discuss how research shows that children's achievement can often be linked to parent involvement. When families work cooperatively with the teacher, the child benefits from consistency and educational support at home and in the classroom. Parent involvement also helps the children feel accepted and encourages the parents to support your program.

10 minutes   Ask participants to suggest ways they have involved parents in their programs or ways they would like to involve them. Write *Ways to Involve Families* on a flip chart and list the suggestions. When they are finished, explain that there are many ways to involve parents, but they have listed some common ones.

10 minutes   Explain to participants that you are going to review some additional possibilities for parent involvement. Ask participants to give examples of why good relationships with parents are important. Discuss why some staff might be reluctant to ask parents to help or to be involved. Help participants see that parents often are interested in being involved but do not know what to do or even if they will be welcome.

Describe how one easy way to involve parents is to ask them to donate items. Point out how parents are usually happy to donate supplies such as empty bottles or paper towel rolls for art projects. Give examples of how, in donating materials, parents can learn about interesting activities they can do at home and support their children's education.

Describe what we mean by an "open-door" policy and why it is important that parents feel welcome at any time their child is enrolled. Emphasize that friendliness and communication with parents is necessary in helping them feel welcome—and feeling welcome is a key component of involvement.

Have each person select a partner. (See tips under "Working with Small Groups and Partners," on pages 20–23.)

10 minutes

Partner Activity: Distribute and review the handout *The Many Forms of Family Involvement*. Review the earlier suggestions from the group written on the flip chart as well. Ask participants to put a check by all events they have done in the past year. Ask them to put a star beside any new ideas they would like to try.

4.2 Focusing on Families

The Many Forms of Family Involvement

EVENT IDEAS

Put a check by all events that you have done in the past year. Put a star beside any new ideas you would like to try. Use this list to plan events for the rest of this year or to make up a calendar of events for the upcoming year.

- ___ potluck
- ___ single-parent support group and social
- ___ Parents' Night open house
- ___ end-of-year picnic
- ___ themed potluck (may be combined with event-related ones)
  - ___ Hawaiian luau
  - ___ Mardi Gras party (a great chance to dress in costume)
  - ___ Western chuck wagon
- ___ morning or afternoon treats (a way to involve parents at drop-off and pickup times)
- ___ muffins, tea, coffee (prepared in advance and served by the children)
- ___ Parents' Art or Play Night (parents get to create art or play with or without children)
- ___ Kids' Night Out (supervised night at the center while parents go out)
- ___ children's entertainment night with movies, art projects, or pizza
- ___ holiday or theme-related event
- ___ celebrations (accreditation, successful events, welcomes, anniversary, group birthdays)
- ___ performances
- ___ children's programs (dancing, singing, skits)
- ___ outside entertainers (puppetry, music, special performances and exhibits)
- ___ speaker presentations on:
  - ___ Supporting Children's Language Skills
  - ___ How-to-Handle Sibling Rivalry
  - ___ Brain Development and Television
  - ___ How to Help Your Child Achieve in School
  - ___ Helping Children through Trauma (national crisis, flood, hurricane)
  - ___ Discipline and Guidance
  - ___ What Does Your Child Need to Be Ready for School

My Other Ideas:

From *Twelve Essential Topics in Early Childhood: A Year of Professional Development for Staff Meetings* by Nancy P. Alexander. © 2008. Published by Redleaf Press, www.redleafpress.org. This page may be reproduced for classroom use only.

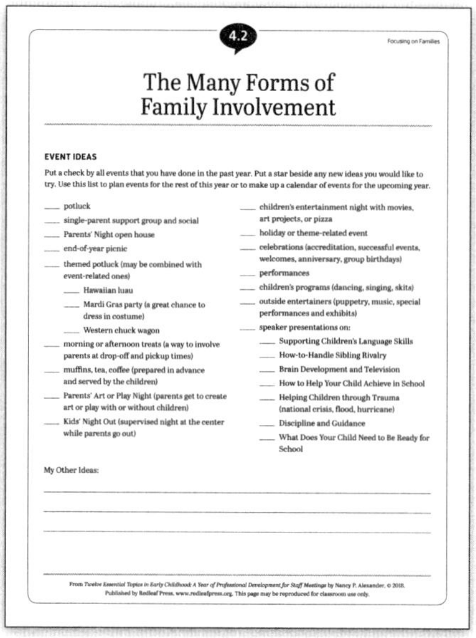

4.2

Distribute the handout *How Will I Involve Families in My Classroom?* Ask participants to select some of the ideas they plan to use and complete the handout to set goals for parent involvement. Ask them to discuss their goals with their partner, and discuss the steps they will need to take to implement their plan.

4.3 Focusing on Families

How Will I Involve Families in My Classroom?

List below some ways that you intend to involve families in your classroom now that you have taken this training:

1. ___
2. ___
3. ___
4. ___
5. ___
6. ___

From *Twelve Essential Topics in Early Childhood: A Year of Professional Development for Staff Meetings* by Nancy P. Alexander. © 2008. Published by Redleaf Press, www.redleafpress.org. This page may be reproduced for classroom use only.

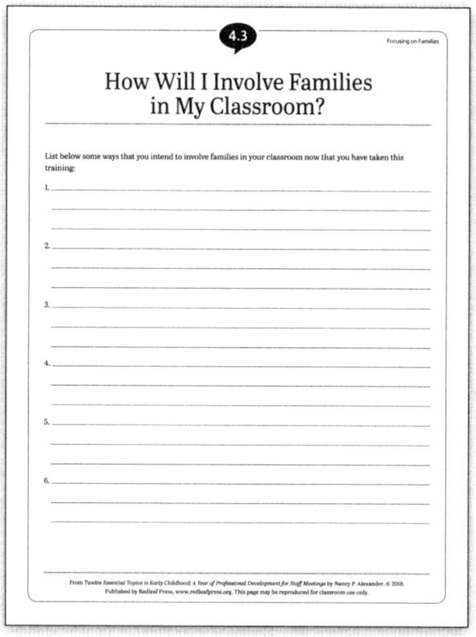

4.3

5 minutes

Conclude the session by reviewing the handout *Top Ten List of What Parents Want from Their Child's Program.*

Ask participants to consider how well they measure up to what parents want and how their involvement plans help meet those needs.

Review and summarize the content of the session.

Distribute certificates if presenting the one-hour session alone.

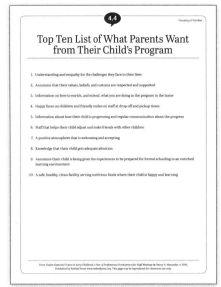

4.4

Second Hour Session

5 minutes

Review the Objectives Part 2. Discuss with the group what they will learn in the session. Ask for specific questions that they want answered during the training.

Objectives Part 2

Describe how to use children's books to support diverse families.

Explain the special needs of some parents.

Describe ways to make parents feel welcome.

10 minutes

Show several children's books selected from the list on page 53 that include diverse families, calling attention to how the books depict the families. Explain how books may be used to help teach children not only that families are different but also that they have many similarities. Read one or two of the books, pointing out how children identify with the characters in the books and build self-esteem by seeing families similar to their own.

Ask participants to review the children's books to see how they depict diverse, blended families; increase self-esteem; and support cultural identity. Tell participants you will leave the books displayed following the session for them to peruse.

Divide the class into groups by the number of children in their immediate family, counting grandchildren. Use categories of 0–1, 2–3, 4–5, 6–8 or more to form the groups. If the groups are not relatively even, ask some people from larger groups to move to a smaller group. Try to have three to six people in each group. If a group is too large, split it into two groups.

10 minutes

Small Group Activity: Select from the following handouts based on which topic is most applicable to each of the groups. Have each group discuss the topic and complete the sheet with suggestions for meeting the identified parents' needs.

> *Involving Fathers and Other Significant Male Figures*
>
> *Special Needs of Grandparents Raising Grandchildren*
>
> *The Needs of Teen and Very Young Parents*

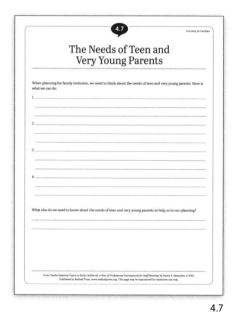

4.5

4.6

4.7

Circulate among the groups to clarify instructions and to provide additional information or suggestions. If one group finishes before the others, suggest they spend the remaining time addressing one of the other handouts. If time permits, let each small group present their ideas to the whole group.

15 minutes   Small Group Activity: Have each group select one of the ways identified in the first hour's *How Will I Involve Families in My Classroom?* Record them on a flip chart so that groups do not duplicate selections. Review the benefits of having parents involved, such as consistency in discipline, modeling how to guide children's behavior, and how parents can learn about child development in order to have appropriate expectations.

Instruct each group to develop a plan to implement their idea of involvement from start to finish. They may create a to-do list; design invitations; or write letters of invitation or announcements. Give them chart paper for their lists, and markers and construction paper for signs or invitations. Remind them that busy parents need simplicity, plenty of notice, and several reminders and various means of communication.

5 minutes   Have each group select a spokesperson to present their project to the class. Offer additional suggestions for each project, recognizing good ideas and creativity. Address any potential problems they might encounter, and help groups identify any missing steps.

10 minutes   Distribute and review the handout *Welcoming Parents Every Day.* Discuss the importance of what a parent sees at drop-off and pickup times. Emphasize that in spite of the time and effort it takes, communicating with parents as they drop off and pick up their children is a key to understanding and cooperative relationships. Ask for additional suggestions of ways to welcome parents. Ask participants to tell about what makes them feel welcome at some of the places they go. Discuss experiences they have had where they did not feel welcome.

4.8

5 minutes — Instruct participants to complete the *Check Your Knowledge* forms by answering the questions again and writing their new answers in the blanks on the right-hand side of the paper. Remind them not to change the answers they gave at the beginning of the session.

Collect the *Check Your Knowledge* sheets, then hand out certificates and any additional information or materials you wish to provide.

4.1

Alternate, Additional, and Follow-Up Activities

GUIDELINES FOR PARENT/ TEACHER CONFERENCES

Distribute and review the handout *Guidelines for Parent/Teacher Conferences*. Discuss how routine parent conferences are a critical means of keeping parents informed and of being active partners in the care and education of their child. Point out that regular conferences are beneficial for all families, not just those experiencing a problem. Ask participants how they might feel as a parent if these guidelines are not followed. Ask them to share some of the benefits of holding parent conferences. Show some sample conference planning forms, invitations, and schedules for routine conferences.

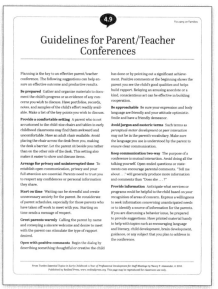

4.9

PARENT PARTICIPATION LIST

Make a list of each child in your class. Beside each name, write how you will involve the family or how you will improve communication with the family.

MORE CHILDREN'S BOOKS DEPICTING DIVERSE FAMILIES

Expand on the activity in the agenda by showing additional children's books that depict diverse families. Ask participants to review the additional books and decide how they might use them to support children's understanding that families are not alike. Ask them to use the books with children and to share their experience at a staff meeting.

Resources

CHILDREN'S BOOKS DEPICTING DIVERSE FAMILIES

- *A Chair for My Mother* by Vera B. Williams
- *All Families Are Special* by Norma Simon
- *All Kinds of Families* by Mary Ann Hoberman
- *Double-Happiness* by Nancy Tupper Ling
- *How Far Do You Love Me* by Lulu Delacre
- *I Love Saturdays y Domingos* by Ada Alma Flor
- *Last Stop on Market Street* by Matt de la Peña
- *One Family* by George Shannon
- *One Love* by Cedella Marley
- *Peeny Butter Fudge* by Toni Morrison
- *Peter's Chair* by Ezra Jack Keats
- *My Family, Your Family* by Lisa Bullard
- *The Family Book* by Todd Parr
- *Who's in My Family: All about Our Families* by Robie H. Harris

ADDITIONAL RESOURCES

▶ Duffy, Roslyn Ann. 2008. *Top Ten Preschool Parenting Problems and What to Do About Them!* Redmond, WA: Exchange Press.

▶ Ernst, Johnna Darragh. 2014. *The Welcoming Classroom: Building Strong Home-to-School Connections for Early Learning.* Lewisville, NC: Gryphon House.

▶ Keyser, Janis. 2006. *From Parents to Partners: Building a Family-Centered Early Childhood Program.* St. Paul, MN: Redleaf Press.

▶ Koralek, Derry. 2007. *Spotlight on Young Children and Families.* Washington, DC: NAEYC.

4.10

Focusing on Families

Check Your Knowledge Answer Key

Mark each answer either T for true, or F for false.

BEFORE		AFTER
	An "open door" policy means parents can pay their tuition when they want.	F
	Research shows that children's education success is not affected by parent involvement.	F
	One way to help build relationships is to address each parent by name.	T
	A good topic for a parent meeting could be how to help children improve language skills.	T
	When we use the term *parent*, we are only referring to the child's mother.	F
	We can help children understand that families are not all alike.	T
	It is not important to involve families unless there is a problem with their child.	F

Write the letter for the best answer for each statement.

One reason for involving parents is ___d___

a. to help children in your center feel accepted.

b. to have consistency in expectations between home and school.

c. to encourage parents to support your program.

d. all of the above.

4.10

CHAPTER 5

Connecting with Children

• Interactions and Relationships •

Materials for Facilitator

▸ Document, Agenda

▸ Document, *Check Your Knowledge Answer Key*

▸ PowerPoint, Connecting with Children: Interactions and Relationships

Materials for Participants

▸ Assessment, *Check Your Knowledge*

First Hour

▸ Handout, *Simple Ways to Build Connections with Children*

▸ Handout, *A Checklist for Interacting with Children*

▸ Handout, *My Plan to Improve Interactions with Children*

▸ Handout, Certificate for Hour One

Second Hour

▸ Handout, *Interacting Scenarios*

▸ Handout, *Specific Ideas for Interacting*

▸ Handout, *What Can I Do?*

▸ Handout, Certificate for Hour Two

Equipment and Supplies

▸ projector and laptop

▸ flip charts or poster boards and markers

For First Hour

▸ flip chart or poster for the Wheel of Fortune icebreaker activity

▸ small prizes, such as key chains or candy bars, for Wheel of Fortune winners

Make-Ahead Materials

For First Hour

Make a flip chart or poster for the Wheel of Fortune icebreaker activity as shown on page 62. Leave space on the chart to write any letters chosen that are not used.

Connecting with Children:
Interactions and Relationships Agenda

First Hour Session

5 minutes   Introduce the topic and then introduce yourself (if working with a group that does not know you).

If planning to conduct the second hour session in addition to the first, pass out the *Check Your Knowledge* sheet to participants and ask them to complete the left-hand side of the sheet. When they finish, ask them to set aside the sheet and not to refer to it until the end of the second session. Tell them that even if they realize that an answer is wrong as they take part in the training, they should not change their answer. This form is to evaluate what they learned in the training and will be anonymous.

5.1

5 minutes   Icebreaker: Wheel of Fortune. Show the flip chart or poster made for this activity. Explain that they will play a variation of the *Wheel of Fortune* television game show and will use words related to interactions. Summarize the directions as follows:

Participants will take turns introducing themselves and naming a letter. Write the letters they select in the appropriate blanks. Write on the chart any letter chosen that does not appear in the words so that it will not be selected again. Ask participants to figure out what the words are that relate to positive interactions. When someone figures out a word, they win a small prize.

Use the answer key on page 62 as a guide for where to write the letters.

5 minutes Review the Objectives Part 1. Discuss with the group what they will learn in the session. Ask for specific questions that they want answered during the training.

> ### Objectives Part 1
>
> Identify outcomes of positive adult-child interactions.
>
> Describe strategies to enhance positive child-teacher interactions.
>
> Evaluate one's own interactions.

15 minutes Ask participants to respond to the following reflective questions one at a time. Once participants have had time to reflect on a question, share as a whole group and summarize their responses on a flip chart.

> Think about the words *kind*, *engaging*, *warm*, *caring*, *calm*, *empathetic*, *supportive*, *positive*, *responsive*, *respect*, and *sensitive* and what they mean to you in relation to your interactions with the children in your classroom. How do these words describe the traits you value in yourself and in others?
>
> How well do you demonstrate these characteristics and support the development of these traits in the children in your classroom? Do you recognize and encourage children when they show these traits?
>
> Would you enjoy your work more if you had ample time for connecting with individual children or small groups during play?
>
> How can you find more time in your daily routines to respond to and interact with individual children? Can you change your daily schedule to allow more time for connecting with children?

10 minutes Brainstorm positive adult-child interactions. Describe how such interactions support brain development and scaffold learning. Distribute the handout *Simple Ways to Build Connections with Children*. Discuss the information on the handout and give examples from your own experience. Explain why each tip is effective. Point out how good relationships support children's learning.

15 minutes   Ask participants to complete the handout
A Checklist for Interacting with Children. Ask
them to think about ways they can improve
their interactions and to complete the
checklist according to the instructions.

They are to put an S in the column if they
seldom meet the guideline, an M if they
mostly meet it, and an A if they always do.

Ask participants to use the form *My Plan to
Improve Interactions with Children* to plan
for improvement of all criteria they rated
S or M. Ask for volunteers to share their
plans and list the suggestions on a flip chart.
Ask them to keep their checklists and their
plans as a reference for the goals they set for
improvement.

5.3

5.4

5 minutes   Review and summarize the content of the session.

Distribute certificates if presenting the one-hour session alone.

Second Hour Session

5 minutes   Review the Objectives Part 2. Discuss with the group what they will learn in the session. Ask for specific questions that they want answered during the training.

> ### Objectives Part 2
>
> Identify ways to support children's feelings and learning.
>
> Use specific phrases that encourage critical thinking skills.
>
> Describe what one should not do in interacting with children.

Divide into small groups of three to six. (See ideas under "Dividing into Groups" on page 20.)

20 minutes   Small Group Activity: Distribute the handout *Interacting Scenarios*. Ask the small groups to review each scenario and discuss the questions at the end of each scenario. If time permits, have them share some answers from their own experience, or have a spokesperson from each small group share the group's ideas with the whole group.

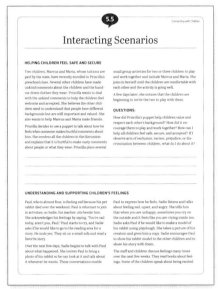

5.5

Have each person select a partner. (See tips under "Working with Small Groups and Partners," on pages 20–23.)

20 minutes — Partner Activity: Distribute the handout *Specific Ideas for Interacting*. Explain to the participants that these are suggestions to help them be prepared for the various types of situations where interactions can be effective. Ask partners to create an additional scenario from their experience for each category of interactions. If time permits, role-play some of the scenarios.

5.6

10 minutes — Partner Activity: Review the handout *What Can I Do?* for suggestions on specific steps to take and what to avoid. Tell them, as partners, to discuss how they will take the suggested steps to improve interactions and avoid undesirable actions. If time permits, ask a few volunteers to share their ideas.

5.7

5 minutes — Instruct participants to complete the *Check Your Knowledge* forms by answering the questions again and writing their new answers in the blanks on the right-hand side of the paper. Remind them not to change the answers they gave at the beginning of the session.

Collect the *Check Your Knowledge* sheets, then hand out certificates and any additional information or materials you wish to provide.

5.1

Alternate, Additional, and Follow-Up Activities

INTERACTION STRATEGIES THAT PROMOTE ACTIVE LEARNING

The adult-child interaction strategies listed below were determined to be most effective in research by the HighScope Educational Research Foundation in Ypsilanti, Michigan. Details on how to apply these strategies, as well as many other adult-child strategies for specific areas of learning, are given in HighScope's training and publications. Review the following strategies with participants and have them identify examples from their classrooms:

Adults participate in children's play. Look for natural openings in children's play and join the play as a partner. As play partners, adults should take roles assigned by children and stay within the play scenario that the children have created.

Converse as co-players with children. Look for opportunities for conversations about the activities. Make comments that allow the conversation to continue without pressuring children to respond.

Use encouragement instead of praise. Make specific comments that encourage children to expand descriptive language and think about what they are doing.

Encourage problem solving whenever possible. While you could often solve a problem easier or faster by taking over, the goal is to help children develop their own problem-solving abilities—and they need opportunities to do so.

In social conflicts, stay nearby to be ready to offer support. Offer support if needed and help children find a solution to their problem. (HighScope Educational Research Foundation 2017)

SELECTING THE BEST RESPONSE

Give participants the handout *Selecting the Best Response*. Ask them to read the scenarios and decide which of the possible responses might be the best response and why. This activity can be an individual, partner, or small group activity. Note: The goal is to consider option— there may be several good responses.

Resources

▶ Burman, Lisa. 2009. *Are You Listening?: Fostering Conversations That Help Young Children Learn*. St. Paul, MN: Redleaf Press.

▶ Dombro, Amy Laura, Judy R. Jablon, and Charlotte Stetson. 2011. *Powerful Interactions: How to Connect with Children to Extend Their Learning*. Washington, DC: NAEYC.

Wheel of Fortune Icebreaker Activity

__ __ __ __

__ __ __ __

__ __ __ __ __ __

__ __ __ __ __ __ __ __ __

__ __ __ __ __ __ __ __ __ __

__ __ __ __ __ __ __

__ __ __ __

__ __ __ __ __ __ __ __ __

__ __ __ __ __ __ __

__ __ __ __ __ __ __ __ __

__ __ __ __ __ __ __ __ __

Wheel of Fortune Answer Key

K I N D

W A R M

C A R I N G

E M P A T H E T I C

R E S P O N S I V E

E N G A G I N G

C A L M

S U P P O R T I V E

P O S I T I V E

R E S P E C T F U L

S E N S I T I V E

5.9 — Connecting with Children

Check Your Knowledge Answer Key

Mark each answer either T for true, or F for false.

BEFORE		AFTER
	Once children know their full names, it is not necessary to use them in conversation.	F
	One way to help children learn positive interactions is to model how to do it.	T
	The only goal of interacting with children is to help them behave.	F
	It is not a good practice to give children choices since you need them to mind.	F
	Teachers can help children learn to recognize and accept their feelings.	T
	If children are progressing well, you need not be concerned about interactions.	F
	Holding engaging interactions can support children's learning.	T
	Asking open-ended questions helps the child's thinking processes.	T

Write the letter for the best answer for each statement.

To increase communication with children **d**

a. talk to children at their level.

b. use children's names.

c. maintain a calm manner.

d. all of the above.

5.9

CHAPTER 6

Guidance That Works!

Materials for Facilitator

- ▶ Document, Agenda
- ▶ Document, *Check Your Knowledge Answer Key*
- ▶ PowerPoint, Guidance That Works
- ▶ Handout, Guidance Word Search Answer

Materials For Participants

- ▶ Assessment, *Check Your Knowledge*

First Hour

- ▶ Handout, *Helping Children Learn Self-Control!*
- ▶ Handout, *Words to Encourage*
- ▶ Handout, *Words That Discourage*
- ▶ Handout, Certificate for Hour One

Second Hour

- ▶ Handout, *Guidance Techniques*
- ▶ Handout, *Guiding Young Children*
- ▶ Handout, *Positive Guidance Includes*
- ▶ Handout, *Guidance Word Search Puzzle*
- ▶ Handout, Certificate for Hour Two

Equipment and Supplies

- ▶ projector and laptop
- ▶ flip charts or poster boards and markers

For First Hour

- ▶ *Words to Encourage* and *Words That Discourage* activity strips

For Second Hour

- ▶ Guidance Discussion Cards Activity
- ▶ assortment of children's books that support appropriate behavior (See list of suggested titles in resources on page 71.)

For Additional Activities

- ▶ assortment of children's books that support appropriate behavior (See list of suggested titles in resources on page 71.)

Make-Ahead Materials

For First Hour

Words to Encourage and *Words That Discourage* activity strips: Copy the handouts on sheets of different colored paper and cut apart each phrase. By making each set a different color, the sets will be easy to keep organized. Put each set of phrases in a resealable plastic bag for quick distribution.

For Second Hour

Guidance Discussion Cards Activity: Print the scenarios and instructions on 3" x 5" unlined white index cards. Print each set using a different ink color to be able to sort them quickly into sets. Print the instructions on a blue index card so groups can easily find the card with instructions. Make one set for each group of three to six participants. Put the card sets in resealable plastic bags for quick distribution.

Guidance That Works! Agenda

First Hour Session

5 minutes   Introduce the topic and then introduce yourself (if working with a group that does not know you).

If planning to conduct the second hour session in addition to the first, pass out the *Check Your Knowledge* sheet to participants and ask them to complete the left-hand side of the sheet. When they finish, ask them to set aside the sheet and not to refer to it at the end of the second session. Tell them that even if they realize that an answer is wrong as they take part in the training, they should not change their answer. This form is to evaluate what they learned in the training and will be anonymous.

6.1

5 minutes   Icebreaker: Adjective Introductions. Ask participants to introduce themselves with an adjective that starts with the same letter as their first name and that tells something about their personality or characteristics. For example, Cathy may be Curious Cathy; Sarah, Sensitive Sarah; or Logan, Loving Logan. Using the adjectives adds humor and makes names easier to remember if the group does not know each other. If they know each other, the activity reveals something about their characteristics. Point out how recognizing children's individual personalities, characteristics, and good qualities are important in positive guidance.

5 minutes

Review the Objectives Part 1. Discuss with the group what they will learn in the session. Ask for specific questions that they want answered during the training.

Objectives Part 1

Describe at least three reasons children need guidance.

Identify at least five personal characteristics important in providing guidance for young children.

Name five ways to encourage appropriate behavior and five ways that discourage.

5 minutes

Ask participants to define what is meant by *discipline*. Write their ideas on a flip chart. Discuss the idea that discipline means punishment to some people, but for the early childhood field, discipline means guidance.

Discuss the importance of providing guidance to young children and give some examples of what happens if we do not help children learn appropriate behavior.

10 minutes

Distribute the *Helping Children Learn Self-Control!* handout. Use this handout as a basis for a discussion of the reasons why guidance is needed and of understanding of guidance as developing self-discipline. Ask participants to give examples from their own experience of instances where self-discipline has been needed for the following reasons:

> wholesome and satisfying relationships with others

> health and safety

> protection of the rights of others

> effective living in a society

6.2

5 minutes

Ask the group to identify what they can do to address each of the common problems for misbehavior. Ask them to keep the handout to refer to regularly as a resource for their daily work.

Ask participants to suggest ideas as to why they believe that children misbehave and what causes the misbehavior. Give some specific examples of situations. Ask participants to share some examples of what they have done to address or prevent misbehavior. Relate the appropriate action with the reasons for misbehavior suggested above.

Divide into small groups of three to six. (See tips under "Working with Small Groups and Partners," on page 20.)

10 minutes Small Group Activity: Ask participants in small groups to brainstorm character-istics of adults who can provide effective guidance for young children. Have each group select a recorder to write the suggestions on a flip chart or poster. After the groups have named six to ten, suggest any from the list below they did not identify. Give some examples of how the characteristics they listed and these below enable an adult to address guidance issues effectively.

knowledgeable about child development

appropriate expectations

consistent in rules

honest and trustworthy

patient and positive

warm and accepting

respectful of children

responsive to children's needs

sincere in affection

actively listens to children

10 minutes Small Group Activity: Distribute the *Words to Encourage* and *Words That Discourage* strips, one set for each small group. Put the strips face down in the center of the group and ask each participant to select one at a time until all are chosen. Have each person in turn read one phrase and let the group decide if the statement is an en-couraging phrase or a discouraging phrase. Have them sort the phrases according to their type, encouraging or discouraging. If time permits, ask them to think of some other encouraging phrases. At the conclusion of the activity, distribute the hand-outs *Words to Encourage* and *Words That Discourage* for them to keep as a resource. Remind them that the encouraging words will go a long way toward helping children learn appropriate behavior and that the discouraging ones build resentment.

6.3

6.4

5 minutes Review and summarize the content of the session.

Distribute certificates if presenting the one-hour session alone.

Second Hour Session

5 minutes Review Objectives Part 2. Discuss with the group what they will learn in the session. Ask for specific questions that they want answered during the training.

Objectives Part 2

Define and give examples of at least three guidance techniques.

Describe at least three positive ways to guide children.

Demonstrate at least three strategies to react to children and help them modify their own behavior by learning self-control.

Divide into small groups of three to six. (See tips under "Working with Small Groups and Partners," on page 20.)

10 minutes Small Group Activity: Describe how teachers who say "please" and "thank you" are *modeling manners*; teachers who compliment children who ask for a turn on the swing are *reinforcing the behavior*; and teachers who go to an area where they notice children are becoming angry are *using proximity control*.

Explain that *planned ignoring* is a deliberate and strategic method of turning one's attention away from a behavior when the behavior is likely attention seeking. Give an example of *redirection*, such as when a child who is marking on a table is given paper to mark on instead.

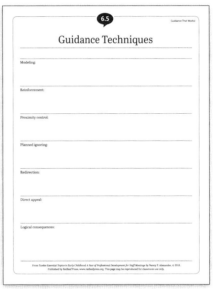

6.5

Point out that *direct appeal* is simply talking to a child and asking for his help in what you want him to do. *Logical consequences* is letting a child experience the consequences of her behavior, such as if she misuses the blocks, she is not allowed to play in the block area.

Distribute the handout *Guidance Techniques* to each person. Ask groups to discuss the techniques and write some of their own examples on their handouts in the space provided. Circulate among the groups to clarify and expand on their suggestions. If time permits, ask each group to select a spokesperson to share one or more of their examples with the whole group.

10 minutes Small Group Activity: Distribute the handout *Guiding Young Children*. Ask a volunteer from each group to read the subtitles to their group or summarize the information to introduce the situations described. Ask all participants to then read the handout and participate in a group discussion.

6.6

10 minutes Small Group Activity: Distribute the Guidance Discussion Cards to each group. (Preformatted text from the Preformatted Handouts folder on the CD-ROM can be printed onto 3 x 5 index cards.) Ask the groups to read and follow the instructions printed on the card. Here are the directions:

6.7

> Each person will draw a card and read the card to the group. In the group, discuss the best way to handle the situation described on each card. Circulate to clarify instructions and provide additional information or suggestions. If one group finishes before the others, suggest they identify and discuss some common situations faced in their classrooms.

The Guidance Discussion Card Activity is provided as a handout option to include written responses.

Have each person select a partner. (See tips under "Working with Small Groups and Partners," on pages 20–23.)

10 minutes   Partner Activity: Show examples of several children's books that support cooperative behavior. Explain how books may be used to help teach children appropriate behavior and support positive actions. Read one or two of the books, pointing out the social behaviors that the books encourage. Tell participants you will leave the books displayed following the session for them to review.

5 minutes   Distribute the *Positive Guidance Includes* handout. Review the information on the handout with the class. Ask for specific examples participants have had with the techniques on the handout.

6.8

5 minutes   Distribute the *Guidance Word Search Puzzle* and let participants work the puzzle. This activity is a review of the material in the workshop.

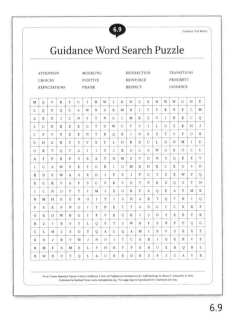

6.9

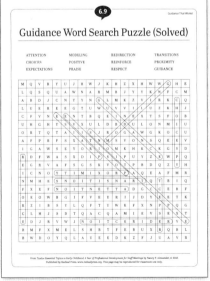

Solved puzzle.   6.9

5 minutes   Instruct participants to complete the *Check Your Knowledge* forms by answering the questions again and writing their new answers in the blanks on the right-hand side of the paper. Remind them not to change their answers they gave at the beginning of the session.

Collect the *Check Your Knowledge* sheets, then hand out certificates and any additional information or materials you wish to provide.

6.1

Alternate, Additional, and Follow-Up Activities

CHILDREN'S BOOKS THAT SUPPORT COOPERATIVE BEHAVIOR

Expand the activity in the agenda by showing additional children's books that support cooperative behavior and allowing time for participants to review them. Ask them to discuss how they might use the books to guide behavior.

UNDERSTANDING BEHAVIOR: A KEY TO DISCIPLINE

Use the handout *Understanding Behavior: A Key to Discipline* as a reading activity. Divide the group into five small groups. Ask each participant to read the handout. Then assign each group one of the five sections of the handout. Ask each group to be an "expert" on that section of the handout. Provide additional resources if any group wishes to explore the topic further. Then have each group select a spokesperson to summarize the information in their section to the whole group.

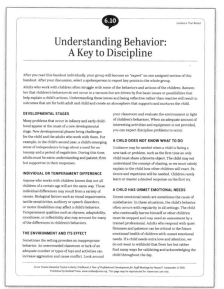

6.10

GUIDELINES FOR DISCIPLINE

Use the handout *Guidelines for Discipline* as a basis for discussion of how to provide positive guidance for young children. Ask participants to give examples from their own experience of ways they have helped children learn appropriate behavior.

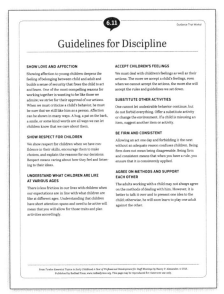

6.11

Resources

CHILDREN'S BOOKS THAT SUPPORT APPROPRIATE BEHAVIORS

- ▶ *26 Big Things Small Hands Do* by Coleen Paratore (Ages 3–5)
- ▶ *Can You Listen with Your Eyes?* by Nita Everly (Ages 3–6)
- ▶ *Can You Use a Good Voice?* by Nita Everly (Ages 3–6)
- ▶ *David Gets in Trouble* by David Shannon (Ages 3–8)
- ▶ *David Goes to School* by David Shannon (Ages 3–8)
- ▶ *Excuse Me!: A Little Book of Manners* by Karen Katz (Ages infant–5)
- ▶ *Feet Are Not for Kicking* (available in board book) by Elizabeth Verdick (Ages 2–4)
- ▶ *Hands Are Not for Hitting* (available in board book) by Martine Agassi (Ages 2–8)
- ▶ *Hands Can* by Cheryl Willis Hudson (Ages 1–5)
- ▶ *I Show Respect!* by David Parker (Ages 3–5)
- ▶ *I Tell the Truth!* by David Parker (Ages 3–5)
- ▶ *Know and Follow Rules* by Cheri J. Meiners (Ages 3–6)
- ▶ *Listen and Learn* by Cheri J. Meiners (Ages 3–6)
- ▶ *No Biting!* by Karen Katz (Ages infant–5)
- ▶ *No, David!* by David Shannon (Ages 3–8)
- ▶ *No Hitting!* by Karen Katz (Ages infant–5)
- ▶ *Quiet, Loud* by Leslie Patricelli (Ages 1–3)
- ▶ *Words Are Not for Hurting* by Elizabeth Verdick (Ages 3–6)

From the Center on the Social and Emotional Foundation for Early Learning's *Children's Book List*. http://csefel.vanderbilt.edu/documents/booklist.pdf.

ADDITIONAL RESOURCES

▶ Burman, Lisa. 2009. *Are You Listening?: Fostering Conversations That Help Young Children Learn*. St. Paul, MN: Redleaf Press.

▶ Bilmes, Jenna. 2004. *Beyond Behavior Management: The Six Life Skills Children Need to Thrive in Today's World*. St. Paul, MN: Redleaf Press.

6.12

CHAPTER 7

Stop, Look, and Learn
• The Value of Observation •

Materials for Facilitator

- ► Document, Agenda
- ► Document, *Check Your Knowledge Answer Key*
- ► PowerPoint, Stop, Look, and Learn: The Value of Observation

Materials for Participants

- ► Assessment, *Check Your Knowledge*

First Hour

- ► Handout, *Why Observe Children?*
- ► Handout, *Observation: The Basics*
- ► Handout, *Types of Observations*
- ► Handout, *Red Flag Words and Confidentiality*
- ► Handout, *Sample Observation Form* (includes two forms per page)
- ► Handout, Certificate for Hour One

Second Hour

- ► Handout, *Using Developmental Checklists*
- ► Handout, *Interpreting and Using Observation Results*
- ► Handout, Certificate for Hour Two

Equipment and Supplies

- ► projector and laptop
- ► flip charts or poster boards and markers

For First Hour

- ► samples of various recording tools (without identifying information) from the handout *Types of Observations*
- ► Observing Others Card Activity
    - ► baby rattle
    - ► three or four small toddler blocks
    - ► crayons and paper
    - ► simple puzzle
    - ► early reader book
    - ► children's scissors and paper
    - ► shoe with shoelace

For Second Hour

- ► samples of child development charts (See list on page 82 for suggestions.)
- ► examples of children's portfolios, notebooks, folders, or online systems

For Additonal Activities

▶ manila folders

▶ pictures/photos

▶ stickers or other items to decorate portfolios

▶ clear contact paper

▶ stapler and staples

Make-Ahead Materials

For First Hour

▶ Prepare a flip chart or poster board with the title How to Observe Children.

▶ Observing Others Activity Cards: Print the statements from *Observing Others Card Activity* on 3x5 unlined index cards and gather the props listed on page 73. A second option is to print 7.6 and glue the statements to index cards.

Stop, Look, and Learn: The Value of Observation Agenda

First Hour Session

5 minutes Introduce the topic and then introduce yourself (if working with a group that does not know you).

If planning to conduct the second hour session in addition to the first, pass out the *Check Your Knowledge* sheet to participants and ask them to complete the left-hand side of the sheet. When they finish, ask them to set aside the sheet and not to refer to it until the end of the second session. Tell them that even if they realize that an answer is wrong as they take part in the training, they should not change their answer. This form is to evaluate what they learned in the training and will be anonymous.

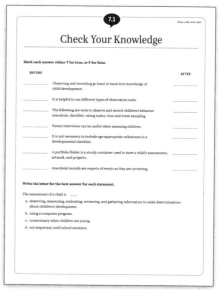

7.1

5 minutes   Icebreaker: Memory. Have individuals face someone they do not know. For 30 seconds, they study each other, trying to remember as much as possible about the person. Then they turn their backs to each other and change three things about their appearance. When they turn around, they try to guess what three things the other person changed. Have participants introduce their partners and tell what their partners changed and how many of the changes they were able to identify. Relate the activity to observing children and how it is difficult to remember everything you see. Explain how it is important that we record significant information about the children in our programs.

5 minutes   Review the Objectives Part 1. Discuss with the group what they will learn in the session. Ask for specific questions that they want answered during the training.

> ### Objectives Part 1
>
> Identify reasons for making observations and recording information.
>
> Describe ways to record behavior.
>
> Identify why confidentiality is important.
>
> Practice using an observation tool.

5 minutes   Ask participants to suggest some of the reasons why observation is important. Write their ideas on a flip chart.

Discuss the values of observing and recording children's behavior. Ask participants to describe any experiences they have had in observing. Ask about what they have learned about children from those observations.

Pass out the handout *Why Observe Children?* Review the handout with the group. Use the vignette in the box of the handout to give a concrete example of how close observation can be used in daily work.

7.2

10 minutes Distribute the handout *Observation: The Basics*. Review the content of the handout with the participants. Point out that this handout provides an overview of the fundamentals of observing children.

Ask participants to suggest ways to record information about behavior that they observe. List their suggestions on a flip chart titled How to Observe Children. When they are finished, add to their suggestions. See the handout *Types of Observations* for ideas if needed. Discuss how observations in all areas of development give us a better picture of the child.

Divide into small groups of three to six. (See tips under "Working with Small Groups and Partners," on page 20.)

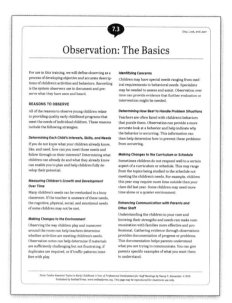

7.3

10 minutes Small Group Activity: Distribute the handout *Types of Observations* and ask each group to review it together. Provide examples of forms or completed observations (without identifying information) for the groups to compare to the descriptions on the handout. Explain how we need to use a variety of observation tools to understand children's behavior.

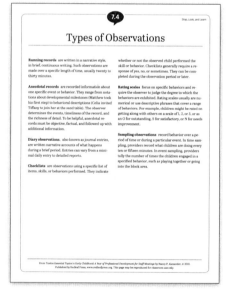

7.4

Ask for volunteers to share any experiences they have had with recording observations, and follow these with a short discussion about what they learned. Discuss the materials needed for observing. Stress that materials are as simple as a notebook and pencil or notecards. Explain how video cameras and audio recordings might also be used.

5 minutes

Small Group Activity: Give each group a copy of the handout *Red Flag Words and Confidentiality.* Allow time for participants to review the information. Give some examples of the types of problems that can be created from inappropriate sharing of information. Relate the importance of maintaining confidentiality to being a professional.

7.5

Have each person in the small group work with the person next to them as partners in the next activity.

10 minutes

Partner Activity: Help participants recognize the importance of being objective and impartial, not judgmental or subjective. Distribute the Observing Others Card Activity materials and the handout *Sample Observation Form.* (Preformatted text from the Preformatted Handouts folder on the CD-ROM can be printed onto 3 x 5 index cards.) Instruct the partners to decide who will be first the actor and who the observer and then to alternate. Give the following instructions:

7.6

Each person in turn will be the actor. The actor will select one of the scenario index cards and perform for the other who will be the observer recording what they see and hear on the *Sample Observation Form*. When the scene is over, observers will compare their observations.

Note: Each page of 7.7 includes two forms to cut apart.

7.7

Each pair will then discuss any opinions or judgments that may have been included in the observations. Then ask volunteers to share some with the whole group.

Note to Instructor: If observations are made objectively, they should be very similar. An observation should be factual. There is no room for opinions, interpretations, or judgments in a valid observation.

5 minutes   Review and summarize the content of the session.

Distribute certificates if presenting the one-hour session alone.

Second Hour Session

5 minutes   Review the Objectives Part 2. Discuss with the group what they will learn in the session. Ask for specific questions that they want answered during the training.

Objectives Part 2

Practice using developmental charts to document children's development.

Identify ways to use observations for planning.

Describe when each procedure is appropriate.

5 minutes   Show some examples of child development charts and discuss how they can help participants see if a child is on target developmentally for the relevant age range. Point out some examples of important milestones in the charts, such as sitting up without support, walking, putting two words together, and so on. Explain how these developmental tasks occur within a general age range in most children.

Divide into six small groups of three to six. (See tips under "Working with Small Groups and Partners," on page 20.) If there are more participants, two groups can be given the same assignment.

20 minutes   Small Group Activity: Distribute copies of developmental charts. Assign each group a developmental area and age group. Each group is to review a checklist for their age and developmental area specified. Here are the categories to select from for each group:

7.8

Physical Development	Infant/Toddler
Social Development	Infant/Toddler
Cognitive Development	Infant/Toddler
Physical Development	Preschool
Social Development	Preschool
Cognitive Development	Preschool

Distribute a copy of the handout *Using Developmental Checklists* and give participants time to review it. Point out the important relationship between knowledge of child development and observation.

15 minutes   Small Group Activity: Have groups find two milestones on their checklists to present to the whole group. They will describe the milestone and how they would determine if a child has met that milestone. Have each group select a spokesperson to present their project to the class. Offer additional suggestions for each project. Address any potential questions they have, and help them determine how they will use the information they have compiled.

5 minutes   Point out how one of the main purposes of observations is to use the information to plan the curriculum. Discuss how one might use information from the activity above to plan experiences for children. Distribute the handout *Interpreting and Using Observation Results*. Discuss the handout information and answer any questions. Explain how parent interviews can add to our knowledge of children for interpreting and using observation results.

7.9

5 minutes   Discuss how information can be stored and what types of items to collect. Show examples of portfolios, notebooks, folders, or online systems and describe the advantages and disadvantages of each. Point out how the portfolios might be used. Discuss the process of collecting materials to include in portfolios.

5 minutes   Instruct participants to complete the *Check Your Knowledge* forms by answering the questions again and writing their new answers in the blanks on the right-hand side of the paper. Remind them not to change their answers they gave at the beginning of the session.

Collect the *Check Your Knowledge* sheets, then hand out certificates and any additional information or materials you wish to provide.

7.1

Alternate, Additional, and Follow-Up Activities

TEACHER-MADE PORTFOLIO ACTIVITY

Each participant will receive two manila folders. They will have a choice of several printed pictures and items to decorate the front of their teacher-made portfolio. Instruct them to open one folder and lay it flat. They are to decorate and label the outside of the folder, then cover it with clear contact paper. With both folders open flat, lay the decorated folder right side up on top of the other folder. Staple the sides and bottom together. This offers a strong and sturdy portfolio to store assessments, artwork, and projects.

MAKING A PLAN FOR OBSERVATION HANDOUT

Cut the *Making a Plan for Observation Handout* into strips so that each strip has one scenario on it. Put each set in a resealable bag.

Pass a set of the paper strips to each group. Ask each person to take one of the strips and read it to their group. Participants will discuss the situation presented and the observation method/tools to best use in each situation. Participants will answer the question, "How can I best observe and record the behaviors of children in these situations?"

7.10

Resources

▶ Curtis, Deb, and Margie Carter. 2000. *The Art of Awareness: How Observation Can Transform Your Teaching*. St. Paul, MN: Redleaf Press.

▶ Feeney, Stephanie, Nancy K. Freeman, Eva Moravcik. 2016. *Teaching the NAEYC Code of Ethical Conduct: A Resource Guide*. Washington, DC: NAEYC.

▶ Fennimore, Beatrice Schneller. 2014. *Standing up for Something Every Day: Ethics and Justice in Early Childhood Classrooms*. New York: Teachers College Press.

CHILD DEVELOPMENT CHARTS AND MILESTONE LISTS

▶ Centers for Disease Control and Prevention
https://www.cdc.gov/ncbddd/childdevelopment/screening.html

▶ Longstreet Clinic
https://www.longstreetclinic.com/pediatrics/child-development-stages/

▶ Noodle Soup
http://www.noodlesoup.com/growthcharts.aspx

▶ Ohio Child Welfare
http://www.rsd.k12.pa.us/Downloads/Development_Chart_for_Booklet.pdf

▶ Pathways.org
https://pathways.org/us/our-mission

OTHER RESOURCES FOR UNDERSTANDING DEVELOPMENT

▶ PBS Parents
http://nunu.pbs.org/parents

▶ Zero to Three
https://www.zerotothree.org/resources/103-9-12-months-your-baby-s-development

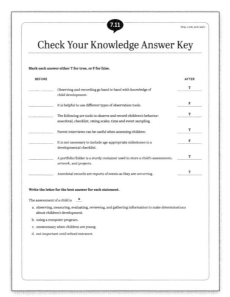

7.11

CHAPTER 8

Creative Indoor Environments

• Room Arrangement as a Guide • to Learning and Behavior

Materials for Facilitator

- Document, Agenda
- Document, *Check Your Knowledge Answer Key*
- PowerPoint, Creative Indoor Environments: Room Arrangement as a Guide to Learning and Behavior

Materials for Participants

- Assessment, *Check Your Knowledge*

First Hour

- Handout, *Advantages of Learning Centers*
- Handout, *Establishing and Arranging Interest Areas: Guidelines to Consider*
- Handout, *Identifying Problems Related to Room Arrangement Activity Sheet*
- Handout, Certificate for Hour One

Second Hour

- Handout, *Evaluating Interest Centers*
- Handout, *The Teacher's Role*
- Handout, Certificate for Hour Two

Equipment and Supplies

- projector and laptop
- flip charts or poster boards and markers

For First Hour

- strips of paper for icebreaker activity
- Tip Bag for icebreaker activity

For Second Hour

- Interest Area Checklist Cards as prepared under "Make-Ahead Materials"
- school supply catalogs
- scissors
- glue

For Additional Activities

- Indoor Environment Tent Cards (See page 89 for description.)
- poster board and markers
- scrapbook materials including a photo of existing room arrangements and the improved arrangements, markers, colored pencils, labels, and paper, or use a digital scrapbook program.

Make-Ahead Materials

For First Hour

Tip Bag for Icebreaker: Purchase or prepare a decorated bag related to the topic of the session or the instructions. For example, a bag with a happy face can be used for "It makes me happy when . . ." See the icebreaker instructions below for more examples. Cut paper strips about 1 inch wide for participants to write their tips and put in the bag.

For Second Hour

Interest Area Cards: Print the Interest Area Checklist Cards on 8" x 5" plain index cards. If index cards are not available, print the information on a sheet of paper, two to a page, and cut apart.

Creative Indoor Environments: Arrangement as a Guide to Learning and Behavior Agenda

First Hour Session

5 minutes   Introduce the topic and then introduce yourself (if working with a group that does not know you).

If planning to conduct the second hour session in addition to the first, pass out the *Check Your Knowledge* sheet to participants and ask them to complete the left-hand side of the sheet. When they finish, ask them to set aside the sheet and not to refer to it at the end of the second session. Tell them that even if they realize that an answer is wrong as they take part in the training, they should not change their answer. This form is to evaluate what they learned in the training and will be anonymous.

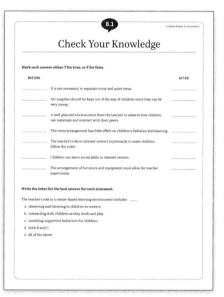

8.1

5 minutes   Icebreaker: Tip Bag. As participants arrive, give them a strip of paper and have them write a tip or suggestion about room arrangement. Relate the bag to the topic of the session or to the instructions. For example, a bag with a happy face can be used for "It makes me happy when . . ." A bag decorated with a telephone can be "Something I want to communicate is . . ." or "I want to ask about . . ." Bags that have "Congratulations" or party decorations on them can be used for "I want to congratulate myself for . . ." or "I want to celebrate that I . . ." As each person puts their tip in the bag, they read it to the group and introduce themselves if they do not already know each other.

5 minutes Review the Objectives Part 1. Discuss with the group what they will learn in this session. Ask for specific questions that they want answered during the training.

Objectives Part 1

Describe the benefits of learning centers.

Name at least five ways that learning centers contribute to children's learning.

Identify and describe at least five learning centers appropriate for preschool children.

15 minutes Distribute the handout *Advantages of Learning Centers*. Allow time for participants to read the handout. Discuss the contents and give some examples of how and what children learn from interest centers based on your own experience. Ask volunteers to share their experiences and ideas about how interest centers benefit children.

Point out how learning centers provide opportunities for child-initiated and child-directed activities—important components of developmentally appropriate programs.

8.2

Have each person select a partner. (See tips under "Working with Small Groups and Partners," on pages 20–23.)

10 minutes Partner Activity: Distribute the handout *Establishing and Arranging Interest Areas: Guidelines to Consider*. Review the suggestions. Ask partners to share their ideas about each statement and to discuss examples from their own classrooms. If time permits, ask each pair to share one of their examples to the whole group.

8.3

15 minutes   Partner Activity: Distribute the hand-out *Identifying Problems Related to Room Arrangement Activity Sheet* to each pair. Instruct them to list problems in the first column, then consider and discuss how the environment may contribute to or cause undesirable behavior. They should then determine how they might change the environment to alleviate the behavior.

Note: A facilitator's aid on page 92 provides suggestions for the instructor.

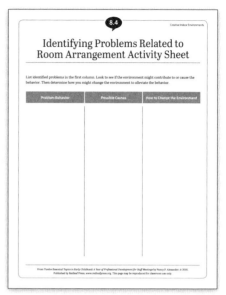

8.4

5 minutes   Conclude the session by reviewing the learning value of interest centers.

Review and summarize the content of the session.

Distribute certificates if presenting the one-hour session alone.

Second Hour Session

5 minutes   Review the Objectives Part 2. Discuss with the group what they will learn in this session. Ask for specific questions that they want answered during the training.

Objectives Part 2

Plan an interest center, selecting equipment and supplies.

Identify specific guidelines for evaluating and improving typical interest centers.

Describe the teacher's role in an interest center.

Divide into small groups of three to six. (See tips under "Working with Small Groups and Partners," on page 20.)

20 minutes — Small Group Activity: Each group will select or be assigned a learning center: art, blocks, science center, dramatic play, library (reading center), manipulatives (table toys). You may substitute music and movement or sand and water play for any above areas, or include them if the group is large. Give each group one of the Interest Area Cards to use as a guide. (Preformatted text from the Preformatted Handouts folder on the CD-ROM can be printed onto 8 x 5 cards.)

Give each group a poster board or large sheet of paper and markers, school supply catalogs, scissors, and glue. Have them create their assigned learning center using pictures from the catalogs or drawings. Ask them to list possible items to include in their centers using the cards as a guide for suggestions.

Circulate to clarify the instructions and to provide additional information or suggestions. If one group finishes before the others, suggest they spend the remaining time discussing variations to their centers.

8.5

10 minutes — Have each group select a spokesperson to present their project to the class. Offer additional suggestions for each project and recognize good ideas and creativity. Address any potential problems they might encounter, and help them determine ways to prevent or address problems. Hold a walkabout where participants circulate to view and discuss the interest centers created by each group.

15 minutes — Pass out the handout *Evaluating Interest Centers*. Allow time for participants to review the handout. Explain that it includes criteria for each typical interest area. Point out that they should keep this handout to use to continue to improve their learning centers.

8.6

5 minutes

Distribute the handout *The Teacher's Role*. Review and discuss the content. Ask participants to give examples of how the teacher interacts with children to support learning.

Explain the concepts of scaffolding and instructional support in children's learning. Discuss how the teacher's interactions during dramatic play time support and guide children's learning.

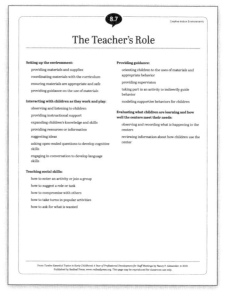

8.7

5 minutes

Instruct participants to complete the *Check Your Knowledge* forms by answering the questions again and writing their new answers in the blanks on the right-hand side of the paper. Remind them not to change their answers they gave at the beginning of the session.

Collect the *Check Your Knowledge* sheets, then hand out certificates and any additional information or materials you wish to provide.

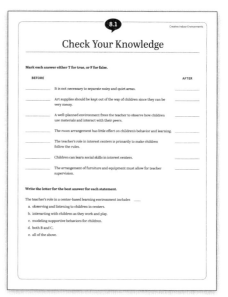

8.1

8.11

Alternate, Additional, and Follow-Up Activities

INDOOR ENVIRONMENT TENT CARD ACTIVITY

To make Indoor Environment Tent Cards, fold paper in quarters like a horizontal greeting card prior to the training. Print one of the topics below on the face of each card. You will need one card for each group of three to six participants. Stand cards like a tent on each table when ready to use.

> Housekeeping/Dramatic Play
>
> Manipulatives/Table Toys
>
> Blocks/Construction
>
> Art/Messy Play
>
> Library/Book Area
>
> Science/Discovery

Each tent card should have the following instructions and questions inside:

> In your group, select an interest center and answer the following questions related to that center to identify how you would set up the area.
>
> > What would you buy?
> >
> > What if you have little money? How will you improvise?
> >
> > How would you let children know where items go?
> >
> > What limits or rules would you have?

Ask small groups to select a learning center and answer the questions on the tent cards. Allow time for each small group to report to the whole group. If working with a large number of participants where two or more small groups may want to select the same interest area, prepare additional tent cards.

ROOM ARRANGEMENT CHECKLIST

Distribute and review the handout *Room Arrangement Checklist.* Ask partners to work together to assess their classrooms, using the checklist. Instruct the participants to put a check by each criterion their rooms meet. Ask them to work together to make a plan to address criteria that their classroom does not meet or that they want to improve and to write their ideas on the lines provided.

8.8

POSTERS FOR COMMUNICATING ABOUT CHILDREN'S LEARNING

Ask participants in small groups to select an interest center and make a poster about what children learn in that center. Display the posters during a break or at the end of a session for everyone in the class to view. Alternately, let each individual make a poster that they can take with them to post in their classroom.

BEFORE-AND-AFTER SCRAPBOOK

Help the trainee make a scrapbook page showing each room area before you begin working with the participant and again after improvements are made. The scrapbook page can be made either manually as a paper notebook or by using a digital scrapbook software program. The trainee can identify and list the problems in the original arrangement and the benefits of the new arrangements. Showing before-and-after photos provides a visual representation and documentation of progress.

SEEING THE CHILD'S POINT OF VIEW

Help participants look at their rooms from the child's viewpoint. Getting on the floor gives one an entirely different perspective of the room. This activity is a good way to point out the importance of where we put displays and items intended for the children and to determine how children see the room. Ask participants what they learn from seeing this point of view.

INDOOR ENVIRONMENTS QUESTIONS

Use the *Indoor Environments Questions* handout to begin a group discussion as a follow-up or to expand on participants' skills.

Use the questions at the top to stimulate discussion.

Ask participants to write ideas they want to try in the space provided.

8.9

GENERAL ENVIRONMENT GUIDELINES

Have participants read through the *General Environment Guidelines* and mark yes or no based on their own environment. Once they have completed the form, have them discuss their answers with a neighbor as a partner activity. This checklist can be used to assess progress in improving one's room arrangement.

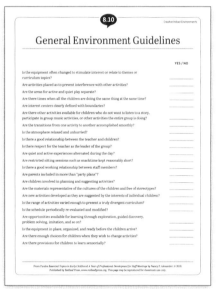

8.10

Resources

► Duncan, Sandra, Jody Martin, and Rebecca Kreth. 2016. *Rethinking the Classroom Landscapes: Creating Environments That Connect Young Children, Families, and Communities*. Lewisville, NC: Gryphon House.

► Isbell, Rebecca T., and Betty Exelby. 2001. *Early Learning Environments That Work*. Beltsville, MD: Gryphon House.

Identifying Problems Related to Room Arrangement: Facilitator's Aid

Below is an example of situations where the environment contributes to problem behavior and how it might be addressed.

Problem Behavior	Possible Causes	How to Change the Environment
Running in the classroom	Too much open space; room not divided into smaller areas; long narrow spaces.	Use shelves and furniture to divide the space.
Fighting over toys	Few duplicate toys; children expected to share too often; not enough toys or interesting activities.	Provide duplicates of toys; show children when it will be their turn (e.g., use an egg timer, a sand timer, or a list with names of children waiting for their turn).
Wandering around; unable to choose activities	Room too cluttered; choices not clear; not enough to do; materials and supplies not interesting or challenging.	Remove clutter; simplify the layout of the room and materials; add more activity choices.
Easily distracted; trouble staying with a task and completing it	Areas undefined and open; children can see everything going on in the room; materials and supplies not set up attractively.	Use shelves to define areas so children are not distracted by other activities; pay attention to the aesthetics of the areas.
Materials used roughly; resistance to cleaning up materials	Materials on shelves are messy; no order to display of materials; materials not cared for by adults.	Make a place for everything; use picture labels to show where materials go; demonstrate and teach care of materials.

CHAPTER 9

Technology Is Terrific!

Materials for Facilitator

- Document, Agenda
- Document, *Check Your Knowledge Answer Key*
- Document, Technology and Children: Teacher Aid
- PowerPoint, Technology Is Terrific!

Materials for Participants

- Assessment, *Check Your Knowledge*

First Hour

- Handout, *Learning and Computers*
- Handout, *Tips and Hints for Using Technology*
- Handout, *Classroom Arrangement for Technology*
- Handout, Certificate for Hour One

Second Hour

- Handout, *Child Projects and Teacher-Made Ideas Using Technology*
- Handout, *Planning for Social Development in the Computer Center*
- Job Aid, *Checklist for Providing Guidance*
- Job Aid, *Checklist for Using Technology*
- Handout, Certificate for Hour Two

Equipment and Supplies

- projector and laptop
- flip charts or poster boards and markers

For First Hour

- Technology Tip Bag
- blank index cards
- Objectives Index Cards
- examples of technology, such as CDs, videos, DVDs, digital cameras, or calculators
- various types of software or apps
- Technology Center Tent Cards
- photos of computer centers or catalog pages showing computer centers

For Second Hour

- *Providing Guidance* and *Using Technology Checklist Job Aids* index cards
- examples of technology such as CDs, videos, DVDs, digital cameras, or calculators
- examples of technology-created projects

For Additional Activities

- Making the Technology Area Work index cards
- photos of technology centers
- materials for teacher-made games and learning materials

Make-Ahead Materials

For First Hour

▶ Technology Tip Bag: Decorate a bag related to technology. For example, use pictures of computers, tablets, cell phones, or cameras.

▶ Objectives Index Cards: Print each training objective on a 3" x 5" unlined index card.

▶ Technology Center Tent Cards: Print tent cards on card stock and fold them like a horizontal folded greeting card. Make one for each group of three to six participants. Stand them like a tent on each table when ready to do the activity.

For Second Hour

Providing Guidance and Using Technology Checklist Job Aids: Print *Providing Guidance and Using Technology Checklist Job Aids* on 5" x 8" index cards, making one set for each attendee. If index cards are not available, the information can be printed using 9.7.

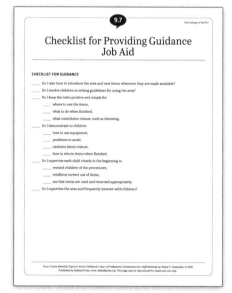

9.7

For Additional Activities

Photos of a variety of technology centers printed or pasted on card stock

> ### Note to Instructor:
>
> Instructors are strongly encouraged to review policies and position statements regarding children and screen time prior to conducting this training. As technology advances, so does our knowledge of best practices in advancing children's learning. Information is available on the American Academy of Pediatrics website and through the National Association for the Education of Young Children.

Technology Is Terrific Agenda

First Hour Session

5 minutes   Introduce the topic and then introduce yourself (if working with a group that does not know you).

If planning to conduct the second hour session in addition to the first, pass out the *Check Your Knowledge* sheet to participants and ask them to complete the left-hand side of the sheet. When they finish, ask them to set aside the sheet and not to refer to it until the end of the second session. Tell them that even if they realize that an answer is wrong as they take part in the training, they should not change their answer. This form is to evaluate what they learned in the training and will be anonymous.

9.1

5 minutes   Icebreaker: Technology Tip Bag. Have participants write a tip about technology, a suggestion about using technology, or a question they have on index cards and put them in a bag. Have participants draw one card each, introduce themselves, and read the tip to the group.

Using the same bag, put in the Objective Index Cards and ask three participants to each draw a card from the bag. Have each participant read aloud the objective on the card. Discuss with the group what they will learn in the session. Ask for specific questions that they want answered during the training.

Objectives Part 1

Describe what we mean by technology.

Identify at least three ways technology can contribute to children's development and learning.

Give at least five tips for arranging, using, and supervising technology in the classroom.

Ask participants to name some of the items they consider technology. Discuss some of the ways technology can be used appropriately with children. Explain that although we will use the term *computer* in many instances for this training, many of the activities would apply to iPads, tablets, cell phones, or other technology that can provide some computer or Internet functions. Additionally, the term *software* will be used but the information would apply equally to apps or online sites that provide similar functions.

5 minutes

Discuss why it is important to select technology items and activities according to the ages and developmental levels of the children. Show some of the various technology items you have brought. Ask participants to describe the benefits to children and the ways the items might be used to enrich the curriculum. For example, a music CD could be used for movement activities when children cannot go outdoors; a computer program might be used to create a book and develop literacy skills; an app might allow a child to make a map of the school.

Have each person select a partner. (See tips under "Working with Small Groups and Partners," on pages 20–23.)

10 minutes

Partner Activity: Distribute the handout *Learning and Computers*. Allow time for participants to review the information and discuss it with their partners. Discuss how planning is important in making computer time effective and integrating technology use with the rest of the curriculum.

Point out that for the purpose of this session, computer refers to a variety of similar devices such as iPads, tablets, and even cell phones.

9.2

5 minutes Distribute the handout *Tips and Hints for Using Technology*. Review the information and answer any questions participants have. Ask for any other suggestions or ideas they have about using technology. Encourage participants to write their additional ideas at the bottom of the handout.

Discuss ideas for introducing items to children. Ask participants to share what they have done and how well it worked.

9.3

5 minutes Ask participants to suggest ideas for software or apps and tell how they have used them successfully in their classroom. Show some examples of software that illustrate the criteria.

Divide into small groups of three to six. (See tips under "Working with Small Groups and Partners," on page 20.)

10 minutes Small Group Activity: Distribute the Technology Center Tent Cards, setting one card on the table of each group. Ask participants to follow the instructions on the tent card and answer the questions in their groups. Ask them to write their ideas on a flip chart if time permits, ask them to share their ideas with the whole group. See the "Technology and Children: Teacher Aid," on page 104, for additional ideas and suggestions to guide the discussion of the groups.

9.4

5 minutes   Show pictures of how to organize a computer center. School supply catalogs or books on room arrangement often have photos of technology centers. Discuss the importance of properly setting up the environment for the effective use of technology. Emphasize the need to have low, open shelves for materials and a table nearby for children to work on. Help participants understand that both the location of the technology center and how the items are displayed influence how the children use, learn from, and take care of the materials. Point out that children need easily accessible materials such as paper and art supplies to use in conjunction with the technology.

5 minutes   Distribute the *Classroom Arrangement for Technology* handout. Discuss the content with the participants and answer any questions about classroom setups. Point out the relationship of how the area is arranged and children's independent use of devices.

Remind participants that the information refers to all electronic devices used, such as iPads and tablets that function similar to computers.

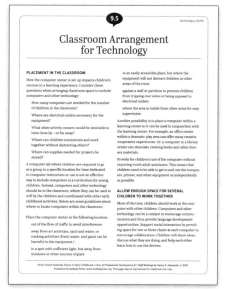

9.5

5 minutes   Conclude the session by reviewing the discussions about arrangement of technology equipment and supplies.

Review and summarize the content of the session.

Distribute certificates if presenting the one-hour session alone.

Second Hour Session

5 minutes   Review the Objectives Part 2. Discuss with the group what they will learn in the session. Ask for specific questions that they want answered during the training.

> **Objectives Part 2**
>
> Name at least five appropriate uses of technology for preschool children.
>
> Identify ways to guide children in using technology.
>
> Describe ways to support social development in technology usage.

Divide into small groups of three to six. (See tips under "Working with Small Groups and Partners," on page 20.)

15 minutes   Small Group Activity: Distribute the *Child Projects and Teacher-Made Ideas Using Technology* handout, one for each group. Show and discuss some of the learning materials that teachers can make with technology. Show some items children have made using technology.

Ask each group to list or describe additional child projects on teacher-made items on the sheet. Allow time for each group to share their ideas with the whole group.

Leave the items for participants to peruse along with the various technology items, catalogs, and information displayed.

9.6

10 minutes   Discuss how one can introduce and provide guidance in the technology center. Distribute the job aid *Checklist for Providing Guidance* and point out how participants can put the job aid in a prominent place near the technology area in their classroom for reference. Point out that they can refer to the job aid as a reminder of what they should do. Discuss the importance of supervision and guidance in the technology center.

Discuss why rules should be simple and few. Ask for suggestions on rules that one might have for a technology center, and list them on a flip chart. If any suggestions are given in negative terms, ask the group to reword the suggestion into a positive statement. Point out the need to supervise the area and interact with children.

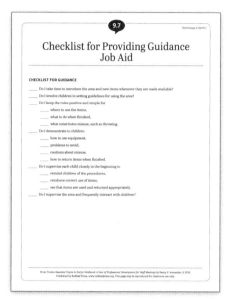

9.7

10 minutes   Distribute the job aid *Checklist for Using Technology* and review the guidelines with the participants. Instruct them to post the job aid near their technology area to refer to frequently as a guide for implementing or improving their technology area.

Ask participants to think about the criteria and how well they already meet the guidelines. Ask them to consider how they will improve in providing for developmentally appropriate learning using technology.

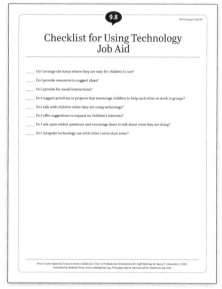

9.8

Have each person select a partner. (See tips for selecting partners under "Working with Small Groups and Partners" on pages 20–23.)

10 minutes   Partner Activity: Show the assortment of technology items again, and review by asking partners to list two types of technology and at least three skills or concepts the item helps children develop and/or what children learn from them.

5 minutes Distribute the handout *Planning for Social Development in the Computer Center*. Discuss how to encourage interactions and conversations while using technology. Remind participants that since many technology uses are lone activities, it is important to look for specific ways to make technology use include social interactions whenever possible.

For example, suggest children help each other and encourage activities where they work with others.

9.9

5 minutes Instruct participants to complete the *Check Your Knowledge* forms by answering the questions again and writing their new answers in the blanks on the right-hand side of the paper. Remind them not to change their answers they gave at the beginning of the session.

Collect the *Check Your Knowledge* sheets, then hand out certificates and any additional information or materials you wish to provide.

9.1

Alternate, Additional, and Follow-Up Activities

MAKING THE TECHNOLOGY AREA WORK

Print the scenarios *Making the Technology Area Work* either on index cards or on paper to cut apart. (Preformatted text from the Preformatted Handouts folder on the CD-ROM can be printed onto 3 x 5 index cards.)

In small groups, ask participants to discuss each scenario, suggesting how each situation might be resolved. This activity can help trainees who already have a technology area to address problems and issues they are having.

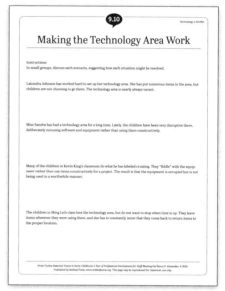

9.10

TEACHER-MADE GAMES AND MATERIALS

As a small group activity, make up simple games that involve curriculum areas and using digital cameras. Or, a group might decide to use photos to make posters of guidelines for classroom areas. They might make a classroom schedule with photos of the different activities, such as morning meeting, outdoor time, lunch. Be prepared to offer suggestions if groups have trouble coming up with their own ideas.

PHOTO CARDS

Take photos of your classroom technology centers. Print them and ask groups to evaluate the areas in the photos and discuss what is right about the areas and what might be improved.

CHILDREN AND CAMERAS

Review the handout *Children and Cameras* and select two or three of the ideas to try. Hold a staff meeting to plan the experiences and another meeting to share how successful the activities were and how children responded.

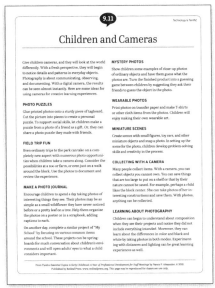

9.11

Resources

▶ NAEYC. Positon Statement *Technology and Interactive Media as Tools in Early Childhood Programs Serving Children from Birth through Age 8.* http://www.naeyc.org/files/naeyc/file/positions/PS_technology_WEB2.pdf.

▶ Simon, Fran, and Karen N. Nemeth. 2012. *Digital Decisions: Choosing the Right Technology Tools for Early Childhood Education.* Lewisville, NC: Gryphon House.

Technology and Children: Teacher Aid

Many types of technology can be used effectively with children. Here are some possibilities:

Recorders Record children reading aloud or telling their own stories, poems, and songs. Let them listen to stories recorded by others.

Cameras Record skits, performances, and presentations on video or take photos. Children can tell a story in pictures and write or dictate the captions.

TV/VCRs Play back recordings of class activities and of tapes that the children have made.

Calculators Let children use calculators in dramatic play and for real tasks such as adding the number of boys and the number of girls to tell how many children are present.

Computers Allow children to access information and explore. They can create, draw and write, and sort and categorize information. Computers can also be used to publish and communicate with others around the world.

9.12

CHAPTER 10

Do the Right Thing

• Ethics and Professionalism •

Materials for Facilitator

- ▸ Document, Agenda
- ▸ Document, *Check Your Knowledge Answer Key*
- ▸ Document, Many Hats Activity Instructions
- ▸ Document, Ethics and Professional Responsibilities Grid Game Instructions
- ▸ PowerPoint, Do the Right Thing: Ethics and Professionalism

Materials for Participants

- ▸ Assessment, *Check Your Knowledge*

First Hour
- ▸ Handout, *Professional Behaviors*
- ▸ Handout, Certificate for Hour One

Second Hour
- ▸ Handout, *Ethical Conduct Code*
- ▸ Handout, Certificate for Hour Two

Equipment and Supplies

- ▸ projector and laptop
- ▸ flip charts or poster boards and markers

For First Hour

- ▸ assortment of hats or index cards with pictures of hats
- ▸ Applying Professional Ethics Scenario Cards Sets #1 and #2
- ▸ PROFESSIONALISM charts

For Second Hour

- ▸ NAEYC *Code of Ethical Conduct* document, found at https://www.naeyc.org/files/naeyc /file/positions/PSETH05.pdf
- ▸ Applying Professional Ethics Scenario Cards Sets #3 and #4
- ▸ materials for Ethics and Professional Responsibilities Grid Game

For Additional Activities

- ▸ paper and markers
- ▸ variety of magazines
- ▸ scissors
- ▸ construction paper

Make-Ahead Materials

For First Hour

Many Hats Activity: If various types of hats are not available, make index cards with pictures of hats on them. See page 117 for suggestions.

Applying Professional Ethics Scenario Cards Sets #1 (10.3) and #2 (10.4): Print the instructions on blue 3" x 5" index cards and the scenarios on white index cards so that the instructions can quickly be found. (Preformatted text from the Preformatted Handouts folder on the CD-ROM can be printed onto 3 x 5 index cards.) Make one set for each group of three to six participants. Put each set in a resealable plastic bag for easy distribution.

10.3

10.4

Write P R O F E S S I O N A L I S M vertically down the left-hand side of flip charts or poster boards. Make one for each group of three to six participants.

For Second Hour

Applying Professional Ethics Scenario Cards Sets #3 (10.6) and #4 (10.7): Print the instructions on blue 3" x 5" index cards and the scenarios on white cards so that the instructions can quickly be found. (Preformatted text from the Preformatted Handouts folder on the CD-ROM can be printed onto 3 x 5 index cards.) Make one set for each group of three to six participants. Put each set in a resealable plastic bag for easy distribution.

10.6

10.7

Spinners for Ethics and Professionalism Grid Game: You may purchase game spinners or make them. If you purchase them, look for ones with four sections that you can write on. To make spinners, cut a 4-inch-diameter circle from poster board and use a marker to divide into four sections. Write the word *up*, *down*, *left*, or *right* in each section. Cut an arrow spinner from poster board, and insert a brad fastener loosely through the arrow and circle so that the arrow will spin.

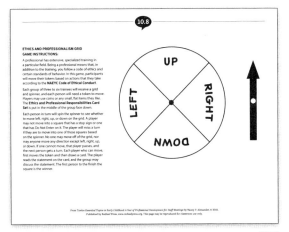

10.8

Ethics and Professionalism Grid Game Boards: Make copies of the board on tagboard, card stock, or other thick paper. Alternatively, you may print on paper and laminate.

Cards for Ethics and Professionalism Grid Game: Print the *Ethics and Professionalism Grid Game Instructions* on a 4" x 6" index card. Print the *Ethics and Professionalism Grid Game Card Labels* document on mailing labels (1" x 2⅝"), thirty to a page. Affix labels to colored construction paper cut 3" x 1½" to make the game cards. Make each set a different color construction paper to make it easy to sort. Store each set in a resealable plastic bag for easy distribution.

Do the Right Thing: Ethics and Professionalism Agenda

First Hour Session

5 minutes   Introduce the topic and then introduce yourself (if working with a group that does not know you).

If planning to conduct the second hour session in addition to the first, pass out the *Check Your Knowledge* sheet to participants and ask them to complete the left-hand side of the sheet. When they finish, ask them to set aside the sheet and not to refer to it until the end of the second session. Tell them that even if they realize that an answer is wrong as they take part in the training, they should not change their answer. This form is to evaluate what they learned in the training and will be anonymous.

10.1

5 minutes   Many Hats Activity: Have an assortment of hats at each person's place upon arrival, and wear one yourself. Encourage everyone to put on their hats. Or give them index cards with pictures of hats. Have participants think of a way that they wear the hat as professional early care and education providers. For example, a provider wears a police officer's hat because she makes sure that the children are safe. She wears a graduation mortar board because she continues to learn. The "Many Hats Activity Instructions," on page 117, gives suggestions for some hats.

5 minutes   Review the Objectives Part 1. Discuss with the group what they will learn in this session. Ask for specific questions that they want answered during the training.

Objectives Part 1

Identify what we mean by being a professional in early childhood.

Describe the responsibilities child care providers have to children and families.

Discuss the importance of how we communicate with parents and others.

10 minutes
Discuss the factors that determine a professional. Ask, "What constitutes a professional in early childhood?" Some participants are likely to mention attire. Emphasize that attire is important, but the other characteristics of professionals are even more important. Ask participants how ongoing training and self-evaluation relate to improving quality in early care and education. When and why is confidentiality important? What is the role of professional organizations in improving quality? What do we mean by *ethics*?

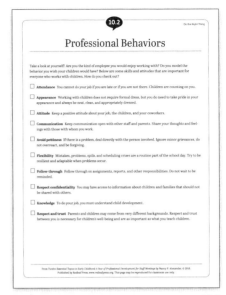

10.2

Ask participants to share experiences where they needed to demonstrate professional behaviors. Following the discussion, distribute the handout *Professional Behaviors* and review any information from the handout that has not been covered in the discussion.

5 minutes
Ask participants to suggest what needs to be done to make early care and education recognized as a professional field. Ask them to identify ways to address areas of needed growth toward becoming a professional. Write their responses on a flip chart. Explain the positive impact on a classroom when staff behaves professionally.

Divide into small groups of three to six. (See tips under "Working with Small Groups and Partners," on page 20.)

10 minutes
Small Group Activity: Responsibilities to Children. Give each group Set # 1 of the Applying Professional Ethics Scenario Cards. Ask for volunteers to read the card with instructions to their groups. Then have volunteers read each situation and the reaction. Discuss what was wrong about each reaction and what would be a better, more ethical or professional response.

10.3

10 minutes   Responsibilities to Families. Ask for volunteers to read Set #2 of the Applying Professional Ethics Scenario Cards. Discuss the difference in how information is worded when talking to families. For example, one might say, "Children learn through play activities. We let them follow their interests," vs. "We let children do what they want."

Ask for volunteers to read the card with instructions to their groups. Then have volunteers read each situation and the reaction. Discuss what was wrong about each reaction and what would be a better, more ethical or professional response.

10.4

5 minutes   Small Group Activity: Give each group a poster board or sheet of paper with P R O F E S S I O N A L I S M written vertically down the left side of the paper. Have the group list a word, phrase, or sentence related to professionalism that starts with or includes a word that starts with that letter. For example, for the letter *P*, the group might list "promotes parent involvement." For the letter *L*, they might list "continue learning."

5 minutes   Review and summarize the content of the session.

Distribute certificates if presenting the one-hour session alone.

Second Hour Session

5 minutes   Review the Objectives Part 2, Discuss with the group what they will learn in this session. Ask for specific questions that they want answered during the training.

> ### Objectives Part 2
>
> Describe the purpose of a code of ethics.
>
> Describe the responsibilities one has to colleagues and society.
>
> Assess one's own professional behaviors.

10 minutes   Discuss the purpose of a code of ethics. Distribute copies of the current *Code of Ethical Conduct* document published by the National Association for the Education of Young Children. Review the sections of the code and distribute the Ethical Conduct Code handout. Have participants answer questions on the *Ethical Conduct Code* handout.

If time permits, ask for volunteers to share some of the answers.

10.5

10 minutes   Responsibilities to Colleagues. Give each group Set #3 of the Applying Professional Ethics Scenario Cards. Ask for volunteers to read the card with instructions to their groups. Then have volunteers read each situation and the reaction. Discuss what was wrong about each reaction and what would be a better, more ethical or professional response.

10.6

10 minutes

Responsibilities to Community and Society. Give each group Set #4 of the Applying Professional Ethics Scenario Cards. Ask for volunteers to read the card with instructions to their groups. Then have volunteers read each situation and the reaction. Discuss what was wrong about each reaction and what might be a better, more ethical or professional response.

10.7

15 minutes

Play the Ethics and Professionaism Grid Game in small groups of three to six. See the game instructions on page 118.

A professional has extensive, specialized training in a particular field. Being a professional means that, in addition to the training, you follow a code of ethics and certain standards of behavior. In this game, participants will move according to actions that they take according to the NAEYC's *Code of Ethical Conduct*.

Each group of three to six will receive a grid and spinner, and each person will need a token or coin to move. A set of cards is put face down in the middle of the group.

Each person in turn will spin the spinner to see whether to move left, right, up, or down on the grid. Everyone starts on the START HERE square. They may not move into a square that has a picture on it. They may not move off the grid, nor may they move any direction except left, right, up, or down. If they cannot move, the next person gets a turn. Each player who can move first moves the token then draws a card. The player reads the statement on the card, and the group may discuss the statement. The first person to the CONGRATULATIONS square is the winner.

5 minutes   Distribute the handout *Professional Behaviors* again. Ask participants to assess themselves now that they have completed this training on professionalism.

Ask them to write a plan for improvement at the bottom of the worksheet. If time permits, ask a few volunteers to share their plans.

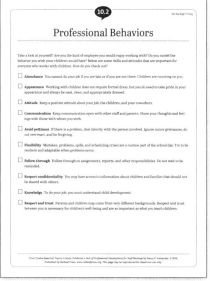

10.2

5 minutes   Instruct participants to complete the *Check Your Knowledge* forms by answering the questions again and writing their new answers in the blanks on the right-hand side of the paper. Remind them not to change their answers they gave at the beginning of the session.

Collect the *Check Your Knowledge* sheets, then hand out certificates and any additional information or materials you wish to provide.

10.1

Alternate, Additional, and Follow-Up Activities

PROFESSIONAL CHARACTERISTICS

Distribute the handout *Professional Charac-teristics*. Explain that this handout enables them to compare the early childhood field with other professions. Ask them to consider the characteristics that are alike. Ask participants to complete the handout either individually or as partners. Allow time for volunteers to share their ideas with the group.

10.9

PROFESSIONAL DRESS PAPER DOLL EXERCISE

Discuss how appearance affects how you and your program will be perceived by par-ents, students, the community, others in the early care and education industry, and perspective clients. Well-groomed employees project confidence and add credibility to their program. Consider how the clothes you wear can affect your work attitude and the program's bottom line. Have groups of three or four people select or design several outfits that would be suitable for early care and education staff. They can cut pictures from advertisements or magazines or sketch their selections. Have the groups share what they chose and why! Write the factors to consider when choosing attire that is listed below on a flip chart:

> ### *Considerations when choosing attire:*
>
> - the organization's total image and level of professionalism
> - the different functions of your job
> - comfort (fabric, fit, make)
> - attractive and flattering colors and styles
> - ability to accessorize easily
> - maintenance and cost

PERFECT PROFESSIONAL

Small Group Activity: Give each group a poster or piece of large construction paper and markers. Have each group create the "perfect professional" caregiver on their posters. Ask them to draw an outline of a person, then list the qualities and behaviors in the drawing or on the side of the drawing. Allow time for each group to share with the whole class. Point out that a professional in child care may not wear a suit, but might wear a name tag, smile, or uniform.

CONTINUING TO LEARN AND IMPROVE

Distribute the handout *Making Good Decisions and Continuing to Learn.* Ask participants to react to the situations and assess what they still need to learn in order to make the best decisions.

Ask them to share some other ideas from their experience and how they handled the situation.

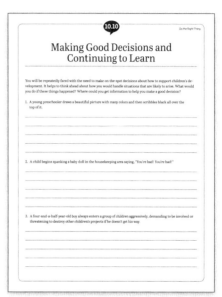

10.10

WHAT IS A PROFESSIONAL?

Divide into small groups and distribute the handout *What Is a Professional?* Ask participants to discuss the handout and how it applies to them. Ask them to give some examples from their own experience about what constitutes a professional.

Note: In these scenarios, there are professional characteristics in all and some nonprofessional attributes. The goal is to discuss the characteristics in the scenarios, not to select one right answer.

Ask participants to answer the questions on the back after reflecting on their own attributes.

10.11

PROFESSIONAL REVIEW

Divide into small groups and distribute the handout *What Is the Professional Thing to Do?* Ask participants to discuss the questions on the handout and work as a group to answer them.

10.12

Resources

▶ Fennimore, Beatrice Schneller. 2014. *Standing Up for Something Every Day: Ethics and Justice in Early Childhood Classrooms*. New York: Teachers College Press.

▶ NAEYC *Code of Ethical Conduct*. 2005, Reaffirmed and Updated 2011. www.naeyc .org/files/naeyc/image/public_policy/Ethics%20Position%20Statement2011_ 09202013update.pdf.

▶ Feeney, Stephanie, Nancy K. Freeman, Eva Moravcik. 2016. *Teaching the NAEYC Code of Ethical Conduct: A Resource Guide*. Washington, DC: NAEYC.

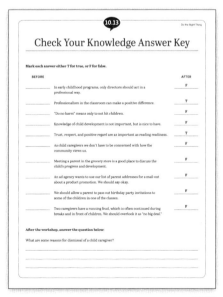

10.13

Many Hats Activity Instructions

Have an assortment of hats at each person's place upon arrival, and wear one yourself. Encourage everyone to put on their hats. Or give them cards with pictures of hats on them. Ask how each hat relates to their job. Here are some suggested answers:

construction hat—building child care; building families

wedding veil or hat—helping parents make the right match with you

graduation cap—providing accurate, up-to-date information about children; having a lot of knowledge and skill

sailor hat—helping parents navigate the sea of subsidies; weathering rough water; running a tight ship

Air Force hat—consulting with military families; being a drill sergeant

baseball helmet—hitting a home run = success; striking out = sometimes failing

old-fashioned hat—knowing the history of the field; exhibiting old-fashioned values

feather-decorated hat—smoothing the ruffled feathers of unhappy parents and dissatisfied staff

firefighter/rain hat—keeping children safe; conducting fire drills; meeting regulations; surviving rainy days; being prepared; saving for rainy day; assisting with natural disasters

football or other helmet—protecting you when you feel you are hitting your head against the wall

magician or leprechaun hat—trying to get money out of a hat; looking for the pot of gold

gardener's straw hat—nurturing children/families and helping them grow

nurse's cap—nurturing children; keeping them healthy; developing healthy policies for your program

hunting hat—finding your target population; hunting for money

train engineer hat—being a leader in "train"-ing

CHAPTER 11

Come Play with Me

Materials for Facilitator

- ▶ Document, Agenda
- ▶ Document, *Check Your Knowledge Answer Key*
- ▶ Document, Selecting Appropriate Dramatic Play Themes Handout Instructions: Teacher Aid
- ▶ PowerPoint, Come Play with Me

Materials for Participants

- ▶ Assessment, *Check Your Knowledge*

First Hour

- ▶ Handout, *The Many Benefits of Dramatic Play*
- ▶ Handout, *Selecting Appropriate Dramatic Play Themes*
- ▶ Handout, *Setting Up a Dramatic Play Dress-Up Area*
- ▶ Handout, Certificate for Hour One

Second Hour

- ▶ Handout, *Suggested Prop Boxes for Dramatic Play*
- ▶ Handout, *The Adult's Role in Children's Dramatic Play*
- ▶ Handout, Certificate for Hour Two

Equipment and Supplies

- ▶ projector and laptop
- ▶ flip charts or poster boards and markers

For First Hour

- ▶ supply of small toys and a large box for icebreaker
- ▶ materials for Matching Response Activity

For Second Hour

- ▶ assortment of children's books that can promote dramatic play (See list of suggested titles in resources on pages 126–127.)
- ▶ prop boxes created from the *Setting Up a Dramatic Play Dress-Up Area* or the *Suggested Prop Boxes for Dramatic Play* handouts
- ▶ materials for Spinner Review Activity

For Additional Activities

- ▶ assortment of hats or index cards with pictures of hats
- ▶ children's book catalogs
- ▶ variety of bulletin board materials

Make-Ahead Materials

For First Hour

Matching Response Activity: Print the scenario and response cards, found in the *Matching Response Cards* document, on 3" x 5" unlined index cards. (Preformatted text from the Preformatted Handouts folder on the CD-ROM can be printed onto 3 x 5 index cards.)

Print the instructions on a white index card. Print scenarios on one color index cards and responses on another color of cards to quickly separate the scenario cards from the response cards. Make a set of cards for each small group of three to six participants. You may also use this as a partner activity by making more sets and giving a set to each pair of partners. Put each set of cards in a resealable plastic bag to make distributing the materials fast and easy.

For Second Hour

Spinners for Spinner Review Activity: You may purchase game spinners or make them. If you purchase them, look for spinners with eight sections that you can write on. To make spinners, cut a 4-inch-diameter circle from poster board and use a marker to divide into eight sections. Write numbers 1 through 8 with one number in each section. Cut an arrow from poster board, and insert a brad fastener loosely through the arrow and circle so that the arrow will spin. Make one spinner for each group of three to six participants.

Print a Spinner Review Sheet on page 128 for each small group of three to six participants.

Come Play with Me! Agenda

First Hour Session

5 minutes   Introduce the topic and then introduce yourself (if working with a group that does not know you).

If planning to conduct the second hour session in addition to the first, pass out the *Check Your Knowledge* sheet to participants and ask them to complete the left-hand side of the sheet. When they finish, ask them to set aside the sheet and not to refer to it until the end of the second session. Tell them that even if they realize that an answer is wrong as they take part in the training, they should not change their answer. This form is to evaluate what they learned in the training and will be anonymous.

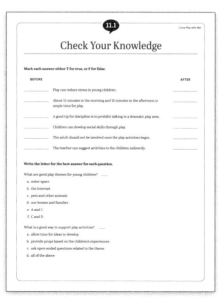

5 minutes What Can You Learn from . . . ? Icebreaker: Have a supply of small toys appropriate for the ages with which the participants work. Place the toys in a box where participants cannot see them. Holding the box high enough that participants cannot see in, ask each person in turn to reach into the box and take out an item. Then ask them to introduce themselves if they do not know each other and to tell something that a child might learn from the item. If anyone has trouble coming up with an idea, suggest that they ask for a volunteer to respond.

5 minutes Review the Objectives Part 1. Discuss with the group what they will learn in the session. Ask for specific questions that they want answered during the training.

> **Objectives Part 1**
>
> Describe four reasons why dramatic play is important to children.
>
> Name four skills that children learn through play.
>
> Select two themes appropriate for preschool children.
>
> Identify five factors to consider in setting up a dramatic play dress-up area.
>
> Demonstrate appropriate responses to play scenarios.

10 minutes Discuss why play is important in children's development. Brainstorm ideas and suggestions about the value of play, listing participants' ideas on a flip chart.

Summarize the suggestions from the group and add any additional suggestions you wish. Distribute the handout *The Many Benefits of Dramatic Play*. Review the handout for additional ideas, and suggest that participants use the handout as a resource for communicating with parents and others about the importance of play.

Point out the need to provide adequate time for dramatic play ideas to develop. Children need 45 minutes to an hour or more to fully develop their play themes.

11.2

5 minutes

Discuss the value of themes and how the teacher can set up materials and props for children to carry out dramatic play roles based on themes. Show items from prop boxes and demonstrate how children might use them.

Divide into small groups of three to six, preferably according to the ages with which the participants work. (See tips under "Working with Small Groups and Partners," on page 20.)

10 minutes

Small Group Activity: Distribute the handout *Selecting Appropriate Dramatic Play Themes*. Explain how themes should be based on children's experiences and knowledge. See "Selecting Appropriate Dramatic Play Themes Handout Instructions: Teacher Aid," on pages 128–129, for ideas and additional instructions. Ask participants to complete the handout, discussing their ideas with their group. Provide time for each small group to share its favorite ideas, and list them on a flip chart.

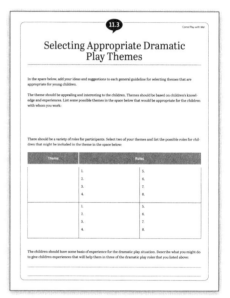

11.3

10 minutes

Small Group Activity: Distribute one Matching Response Activity card set to each small group. Have them read the instruction card and complete the activity to give participants experience in responding appropriately to children's role-play scenarios. Point out that these responses guide children's behavior, expand their knowledge, and support more in-depth dramatic play. If time permits, allow some participants to share their experiences with the whole group.

11.4

5 minutes Distribute the handout *Setting Up a Dramatic Play Dress-Up Area*. Review the content with participants. Point out that the handout provides information that will help their dramatic play area be attractive to children and hold their attention. Ask participants to share additional ideas for items to use in a dramatic play area. Ask participants to save it as a resource of ideas.

11.5

5 minutes Review and summarize the content of the session.

Distribute certificates if presenting the one-hour session alone.

Second Hour Session

5 minutes Review the Objectives Part 2. Discuss with the group what they will learn in the session. Ask for specific questions that they want answered during the training.

Objectives Part 2

Describe how to create and use appropriate dramatic play prop boxes.

Name three books that stimulate dramatic play.

Identify four ways for adults to support dramatic play.

15 minutes Show an assortment of books to stimulate dramatic play that can lead to re-enactments of the story. Explain how reading the story and providing the necessary props will indirectly suggest play ideas to children. Read one or two of the books and discuss what children might do after they hear the story.

Divide into small groups of three to six. (See tips under "Working with Small Groups and Partners," on page 20.)

15 minutes   Small Group Activity: Show several prop boxes selected from the handouts *Setting Up a Dramatic Play Dress-Up Area* or *Suggested Prop Boxes for Dramatic Play*. Discuss how prop boxes are an easy way to organize materials for dramatic play. Have participants select a theme and make a list of props related to their specific theme. After the groups have completed the activity, distribute the handout *Suggested Prop Boxes for Dramatic Play*. Suggest that participants keep the handout as a source of additional ideas for prop boxes.

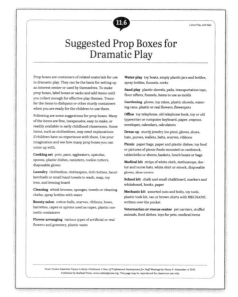

11.6

10 minutes   Small Group Activity: Use the handout *The Adult's Role in Children's Dramatic Play* as the basis for discussing in depth how adults can stimulate children's ideas, conversation, and learning. Discuss how the adult can take part in the play activities by taking on a role. The teacher can suggest ideas but should be careful not to take over and direct the play. Ask the groups to answer the questions on the handout. If time permits, ask volunteers to share their favorite ideas.

11.7

10 minutes   Small Group Activity: Distribute the materials for the Spinner Review Activity. This activity provides an opportunity for the instructor to assess the understanding of the participants while they discuss the answers to the questions. See pages 127–128 for instructions.

5 minutes   Instruct participants to complete the *Check Your Knowledge* forms by answering the questions again and writing their new answers in the blanks on the right-hand side of the paper. Remind them not to change their answers they gave at the beginning of the session.

Collect the *Check Your Knowledge* sheets, then hand out certificates and any additional information or materials you wish to provide.

11.1

Alternate, Additional, and Follow-Up Activities

WHAT I REMEMBER . . . ICEBREAKER

Ask participants to think about their own childhoods and something they liked to play. Allow them to share their early memories about play as they introduce themselves. If the group is large, make the introductions in small groups. When participants mention a dramatic play activity, call attention to how they have remembered it for so long because it was very important to them. Ask them to tell about some of the things they learned from the dramatic play activity.

HAT PROPS FOR THEMES

Items needed:

▶ A variety of hats or 3" x 5" index cards with pictures of hats

Use actual hats if available. If you do not have a collection of hats, make a set of index cards printed with pictures of hats. To make the index cards, print out clip art found on the Internet, and cut and paste each hat on an index card. Or attach stickers or photos of hats on index cards.

Pass out a hat or hat card to each participant. Alternatively, ask each participant to pick a card and tell about a play theme to which that hat relates. For example, a train engineer's hat can relate to a transportation theme; a firefighter's helmet could relate to a community helper or safety theme; a cook's hat to a restaurant theme; or a gardener's hat could be a prop for a gardening play theme.

PARENT LETTER TO REQUEST PROPS

Help participants develop a letter to request prop items from parents and other staff. Review safety and sanitation issues related to used or recycled items. In a week or two, check with the participants to see what items have been received. Make suggestions on how the items might be used or other items that might be requested.

SELECTING BOOKS TO SUPPORT PLAY

Show some of the books from the list below and discuss how the books can stimulate dramatic play. Assist the participants in selecting children's picture books from their own libraries or from the public library that they feel support dramatic play. Help them review catalogs for possible purchases that will be appropriate for stimulating dramatic play. Provide the participants with a list of suggested books if needed.

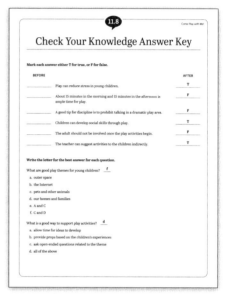

11.8

POSTER OR BULLETIN BOARD

Suggest that the participant make a bulletin board or poster to inform parents about what children learn through dramatic play. Offer materials to assist in creating the bulletin board.

Resources

CHILDREN'S BOOKS THAT ENCOURAGE DRAMATIC PLAY

▸ *Blueberries for Sal* by Robert McCloskey

▸ *Caps for Sale* by Esphyr Slobodkina

▸ *Curious George* by H. A. Rey and Margret Rey

▸ *We're Going on a Bear Hunt* by Helen Oxenbury and Michael Rosen

▸ *Goodnight Moon* by Margaret Wise Brown

▸ *Green Eggs and Ham* by Dr. Seuss

▸ *If You Give a Mouse a Cookie* by Laura Numeroff

▸ *Madeline* by Ludwig Bemelmans

▸ *Make Way for Ducklings* by Robert McCloskey

- *No, David!* by David Shannon
- *Owl Moon* by Jane Yolen
- *Stellaluna* by Janell Cannon
- *Sylvester and the Magic Pebble* by William Steig
- *The Hat* by Jan Brett
- *The Keeping Quilt* by Patricia Polacco
- *The Little Engine That Could* by Watty Piper
- *The Mitten* by Jan Brett
- *The Other Side* by Jacqueline Woodson
- *The Snowman* by Raymond Briggs
- *The Very Hungry Caterpillar* by Eric Carle
- *Today Is Monday* by Eric Carle
- *Where the Wild Things Are* by Maurice Sendak

RESOURCES FOR PLANNING FOR DRAMATIC PLAY

- *Playing to Learn* by Carol Seefeldt—Seefeldt provides age-appropriate activities to demonstrate how children learn by playing games, and by playing with each other and in small groups.
- *Children's Play: The Roots of Reading* by Edward F. Zigler, Dorothy G. Singer, and Sandra J. Bishop-Josef—Leading experts examine the importance of play in helping children learn literacy skills, social awareness, and creative problem solving.
- *Making Make-Believe: Fun Props, Costumes and Creative Play Ideas* by MaryAnn F. Kohl—Explore the world of make-believe with fun and easy-to-make props and costumes.
- *Pathways to Play: Developing Play Skills in Young Children* by Sandra Heidemann and Deborah Hewitt—This essential new work shows teachers how to help children to grow in social competency by developing cooperative play skills.
- *The Genius of Play: Celebrating the Spirit of Childhood* by Sally Jenkinson—The secrets of play are explored through down-to-earth stories as well as through research.
- *Prop Box Play: 50 Themes to Inspire Dramatic Play* by Ann Barbour and Blanche Desjean-Perrotta—Prop boxes contain dramatic play props that offer children the freedom to express themselves and to exercise their imaginations.

Spinner Review Activity

Items needed for each group:

▶ review questions printed on index cards

▶ spinner with eight segments each numbered (purchased or teacher made). See "Make-Ahead Materials" on page 120 for instructions in making a spinner.

See "Make-Ahead Materials" on page 120

Instructions for Spinner Review

Provide each group with a spinner and the Spinner Review Sheet. Each person in turn spins the spinner and responds to the question corresponding to that number. A participant may not repeat an answer that has already been given but must give a different answer. Continue until everyone has had at least two turns.

1. Tell one benefit of dramatic play.

2. Name a dramatic play theme and three props to use with the theme.

3. Suggest an appropriate interaction when two children want to be the cook in a restaurant.

4. Give an example of a social skill children learn through play.

5. Give a tip for setting up a dramatic play area.

6. Describe a teacher's role in play.

7. Name an article of clothing that makes a good dress-up item for dramatic play.

8. Tell one way that language skills increase through dramatic play.

Variation for advanced students or a longer session Make another list of eight questions. After a group has addressed each of the above eight questions, give them a second sheet with the additional questions to continue the activity.

Variation for beginners or for a shorter session Use only four or six questions and a spinner with four or six sections. Or use as a partner activity.

Selecting Appropriate Dramatic Play Themes
Handout Instructions: Teacher Aid

Divide into groups according to the ages with which the participants work. Instruct them to add their ideas and suggestions to the general guidelines for selecting appropriate themes on the handout. If needed, give them an example for each guideline to help them get started.

The theme should be appealing and interesting to the children. List some possible themes in the space below that would be appropriate for the children with whom you work:

Describe some of the topics that usually interest children, such as toys, families, transportation, animals, clothing, and food. Give a few examples from your experience of successful dramatic play themes and why they were appropriate. Discuss how themes for dramatic play must be something that the children know about and that is relevant to them.

There should be a variety of roles for participants. Select two of your themes and list the possible roles for children that might be included in the theme in the space below:

Describe how additional roles might be added to a play theme to include more participation. Discuss how there can be several shoppers, workers, or family members to include more children in a play theme. Share some personal experiences of how a suggestion from you has added roles. For example, in a group of children playing grocery store, when another child wanted to join the play, the teacher suggested that perhaps they needed a repair technician to work on the cash register and scanner, thus creating a role for the child who wanted to be a part of the play. The teacher could also have pointed out that there is often more than one cashier in a store.

The children should have some basis of experience for the dramatic play situation. Describe what you might do that will help them in three of the dramatic play roles that you listed above:

Describe how a specific experience can lead to dramatic play themes. For example, a trip to a fire station will give children knowledge of how firefighters work, which will therefore stimulate ideas for play. Note how this is a good dramatic play theme for outdoors, making use of tricycles and wagons. Or explain how a field trip to a grocery store to purchase a pumpkin will suggest roles of farmers, buyers, and sellers.

    Other activities that stimulate dramatic play could be reading books about the topic, having a visitor bring items for the children to explore, or re-creating experiences the children had in the community when taking part in special events. Even a walk around the block can suggest themes if children see construction sites, repair technicians, delivery trucks, and other people and places.

Let's Go Outside

Materials for Facilitator

- ▸ Document, Agenda
- ▸ Document, *Check Your Knowledge Answer Key*
- ▸ PowerPoint, Let's Go Outside

Materials for Participants

- ▸ Assessment, *Check Your Knowledge*

First Hour

- ▸ Handout, *Why Outdoor Play Is Important*
- ▸ Handout, *Suggested Play Areas*
- ▸ Handout, *Outdoor Activity Areas*
- ▸ Handout, Certificate for Hour One

Second Hour

- ▸ Handout, *Integrating Outdoor Play with Other Curriculum Areas*
- ▸ Handout, *Outdoor Time Tips*
- ▸ Handout, Certificate for Hour Two

Equipment and Supplies

- ▸ projector and laptop
- ▸ flip charts or poster boards and markers

For First Hour

- ▸ school supply catalogs that include playground equipment
- ▸ play money sets of $5,000 for each group of three to six participants
- ▸ scissors, glue, and tape

For Second Hour

- ▸ assortment of children's books related to outdoor play (See list of suggested titles in resources on pages 138–139.)

For Additional Activities

- ▸ pipe cleaners, crepe paper, cardboard, and other materials to make miniature outdoor equipment

131

Let's Go Outside Agenda

First Hour Session

5 minutes   Introduce the topic and then introduce yourself (if working with a group that does not know you).

If planning to conduct the second hour session in addition to the first, pass out the *Check Your Knowledge* sheet to participants and ask them to complete the left-hand side of the sheet. When they finish, ask them to set aside the sheet and not to refer to it until the end of the second session. Tell them that even if they realize that an answer is wrong as they take part in the training, they should not change their answer. This form is to evaluate what they learned in the training and will be anonymous.

12.1

10 minutes   Icebreaker: Childhood Memories. Ask participants to introduce themselves and tell about an outdoor activity that they enjoyed as a child. If they know each other, they can omit the introduction and simply describe what they enjoyed. Usually they will identify creative play outdoors such as building forts or playhouses on vacant lots. Point out how people usually remember creative activities and the activities involving others rather than expensive playground equipment. Explain that they will learn some creative and inexpensive activities for outdoor time in this workshop.

5 minutes   Review the Objectives Part 1. Discuss with the group what they will learn in the session. Ask for specific questions that they want answered during the training.

Objectives Part 1

Describe why outdoor play is important for young children.

Identify materials and equipment that can be provided to stimulate development and learning.

Select equipment for various areas of a playground.

10 minutes Have participants discuss what children gain from outdoor play and how it benefits them. List their ideas on a flip chart and identify the domains of development.

Distribute the handout *Why Outdoor Play Is Important* for participants to write down what is discussed in this and the following section. Point out that this completed handout can be a good source of ideas for communicating with parents.

12.2

Give several examples of outdoor activities that support development in each of the areas. Ask participants to share some of their ideas and experiences. Stress the importance of outdoor time in reducing the problem of childhood obesity. Help participants understand that outdoor time is an important component of the curriculum. Give some examples of how outdoor time can include cognitive skills. For example, pulling a heavy wagon up a ramp or figuring out how to pack sand to make it hold together can help develop problem-solving skills.

10 minutes Distribute the handout *Suggested Play Areas*. Relate the outdoor area to the indoor area, and give examples of how common indoor interest areas can be set up outdoors. For example, an outdoor area can be set aside for reading, and an easel can be set up to make an art area. Dramatic play can be fun outdoors with tricycles and wagons used as vehicles for play themes.

12.3

Discuss what one can do with limited outdoor space and equipment. Ask participants to think about their own playgrounds and what they might change or add to create play areas.

Divide into small groups of three to six. (See tips under "Working with Small Groups and Partners," on page 20.)

15 minutes   Small Group Activity: Give each group an *Outdoor Activity Areas* handout, a set of play money that equals $5,000, some school supply catalogs, and a piece of flip chart paper or poster board. Have each group look through catalogs and cut out what they would like to have on their playground. Each group must not spend more than the $5,000 they were given, but they must select equipment in each of the required areas.

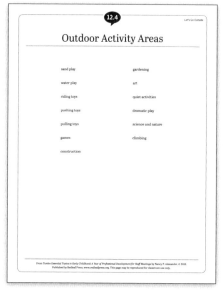

12.4

Call attention to the costs, explaining that equipment intended to be used by many children will need to be sturdier and more durable than items intended for a family's backyard. Explain the importance of viewing equipment as an investment in how long it lasts rather than simply looking at the initial cost.

Groups can glue or tape their items to the flip chart or poster board to make a playground, giving consideration to the arrangement of items on the playground. Ask them to plan for issues such as traffic patterns, protection from the sun, water activities, and storage. If time permits, include a walkabout where each group can view and discuss the other groups' work.

5 minutes   Review and summarize the content of the session.

Distribute certificates if presenting the one-hour session alone.

Second Hour Session

5 minutes | Review the Objectives Part 2. Discuss with the group what they will learn in the session. Ask for specific questions that they want answered during the training.

> ### Objectives Part 2
>
> Make use of outdoor time by integrating curriculum areas.
>
> Describe guidelines for supervision outdoors.
>
> Identify picture books that stimulate creative outdoor play.

15 minutes | Distribute the handout *Integrating Outdoor Play with Other Curriculum Areas.* Ask participants to read these ideas, then list at least three of their own ideas and the curriculum area that their ideas are reinforcing.

Remind them how many activities commonly done indoors can be conducted outdoors and that interest centers can be set up outside just as indoors.

Point out how outdoor time can provide opportunities to expand and enrich the curriculum.

Ask participants to add their own suggestions and ideas of activities in the space provided.

12.5

Point out how nature's sounds can be soothing; thus reading, listening to stories, and just relaxing can be good activities for outdoors. Give examples of how messy art activities might be better outdoors and reduce cleanup time. For example, easel painting outdoors means spills are not a problem, and fingerpainting on a table outdoors is easy to clean up.

10 minutes   Distribute the handout *Outdoor Time Tips*. Give participants time to review it. Discuss the content in the handout.

Ask participants to select some activities to try in the next few weeks and write them on the handout. Explain the value of "loose parts" that children can move and use in a variety of ways. Give some examples of what we consider loose parts, such as cones, blocks, or cardboard boxes. Ask for other suggestions of loose parts they might use.

12.6

Divide into small groups of three to six. (See tips under "Working with Small Groups and Partners," on page 20.)

15 minutes   Small Group Activity: Ask participants to work in small groups to make a list of guidelines for teachers when supervising outdoor time. Provide flip chart pages for them to record their suggestions. Post the flip chart pages around the room and provide time for each group to report to the whole group. Add any suggestions of your own that the groups did not think of.

Have each person select a partner. (See tips under "Working with Small Groups and Partners," on pages 20–23.)

10 minutes   Partner Activity: Show several children's books that could stimulate outdoor play (a suggested list is provided on pages 138–139). Explain how books may be used to give children ideas for outdoor play. Read one or two of the books, pointing out the types of outdoor play that the books encourage. Explain how a book such as *Diary of a Worm* can motivate children to dig for worms. A book like *Nicky, the Nature Detective* can encourage dramatic play as well as an appreciation of nature.

Ask partners to review a book and decide how they might use it to inspire outdoor play. Tell participants you will leave the books displayed following the session for them to review.

5 minutes Instruct participants to complete the *Check Your Knowledge* forms by answering the questions again and writing their new answers in the blanks on the right-hand side of the paper. Remind them not to change their answers they gave at the beginning of the session.

Collect the *Check Your Knowledge* sheets, then hand out certificates and any additional information or materials you wish to provide.

12.1

Alternate, Additional, and Follow-Up Activities

PLANNING A PLAYGROUND

Small Group Activity: Provide materials such as pipe cleaners, crepe paper, and cardboard to make miniature outdoor equipment. Participants can choose from the materials available to explore and make outdoor play materials. Suggest that they refer to their handout *Suggested Play Areas* for ideas of items to make. Provide poster board or large sheets of paper to plan a playground and place their items.

INTEGRATING CURRICULUM

Make a list of common curriculum themes used by your program. Think of two outdoor activities that relate to the themes. For example, tricycles and wagons can be used as vehicles for a community helper theme. Fingerpainting outdoors can relate to a five senses theme.

Variation: Think of two outdoor activities that develop skills or concepts from each curriculum area. For example, using shapes to make an obstacle course relates to math; planting a garden builds an understanding of science and nutrition.

MY WATER AND SAND PLAY

Ask participants to select one of the water play activities and one of the sand play activities from *Outdoor Time Tips*. Have them implement the activity and use the handout *My Water Activity* and *My Sand Activity* to report on their projects.

12.6

12.7

12.8

Resources

CHILDREN'S BOOKS RELATED TO OUTDOOR PLAY

▸ *All Aboard! National Parks: A Wildlife Primer* by Hailey Meyers and Kevin Meyers

▸ *All the World* by Liz Garton Scanlon

▸ *Animals in Winter* by Henrietta Bancroft and Richard G. Van Gelder

- *Before Morning* by Joyce Sidman
- *Best Friends for Frances* by Russell Hoban
- *Diary of a Worm* by Doreen Cronin
- *Enemy Pie* by Derek Munson
- *How Things Work in the Yard* by Lisa Campbell Ernst
- *I Like Bugs* by Margaret Wise Brown
- *Linnea's Almanac* by Cristina Bjork
- *Little Owl's Day* by Divya Srinivasan
- *Nicky the Nature Detective* by Ulf Svedberg, translated by Ingrid Selberg
- *Now It's Fall* by Lois Lenski
- *Our Great Big Backyard* by Laura Bush and Jenna Bush Hager
- *Outside Your Window: A First Book of Nature* by Nicola Davies
- *Red Leaf, Yellow Leaf* by Lois Ehlert
- *Step Gently Out* by Helen Frost
- *The Carrot Seed* by Ruth Krauss
- *The Great Kapok Tree: A Tale of the Amazon Rain Forest* by Lynne Cherry
- *The Snowy Day* by Ezra Jack Keats
- *The Very Busy Spider* by Eric Carle
- *Wangari's Trees of Peace: A True Story from Africa* by Jeanette Winter
- *You Can Be a Nature Detective* by Peggy Kochanoff

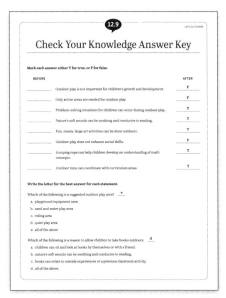

12.9

CHAPTER 13

Super Science FUN!

Materials for Facilitator

- ▸ Document, Agenda
- ▸ Document, *Check Your Knowledge Answer Key*
- ▸ Document, *Icebreaker Instructions*
- ▸ Document, Guidelines for Selecting Science Materials: Teacher Aid
- ▸ Document, Integrating Science into the Curriculum: Teacher Aid
- ▸ PowerPoint, Super Science FUN!

Materials for Participants

- ▸ Assessment, *Check Your Knowledge*

First Hour

- ▸ Handout, *Lucky 13 Key Points Science Worksheet*
- ▸ Handout, *What Is Science?*
- ▸ Handout, *Suggested Science Center Materials*
- ▸ Handout, Certificate for Hour One

Second Hour

- ▸ Handout, *Science Activities*
- ▸ Handout, *The Teacher's Role in Science*
- ▸ Document, Certificate for Hour Two

Equipment and Supplies

- ▸ projector and laptop
- ▸ flip chart or poster board and markers

For First Hour

- ▸ icebreaker materials
- ▸ Feely Bags

For Second Hour

- ▸ assortment of children's picture books with science concepts (See list of suggested titles in resources on pages 149–150.)
- ▸ materials for five activities from the *Science Activities* handout

For Additional Activities

- ▸ children's science books, nonfiction and storybooks
- ▸ materials for activities in *Five Senses Activities*

Make-Ahead Materials

For First Hour

Icebreaker Activity: Place a variety of items, such as cotton swabs, rubber bands, paper clips, crayons, coins, or other small trinkets, in resealable plastic bags. Make enough for each group of three to six participants to have a bag and for each person in the group to have an item. Print the *Icebreaker Instructions* document on index cards and insert one card in each bag.

Science Center Goals Flip Chart: Prepare a flip chart or poster with the following information:

- Acquire basic concepts by exploration and experimentation.
- Develop an awareness of the environment.
- Develop skills in identifying and solving problems.
- Learn to formulate and test hypotheses and draw conclusions.
- Develop units of measure.
- Participate in proper handling and care of plants and animals.
- Manipulate equipment and materials by engaging in various methods of discovery with others.
- Discuss plans; share ideas of discovery with others.
- Develop positive attitudes toward living things, their interrelationships, and our environment.
- Develop classification skills.
- Learn the vocabulary of science.

Feely Bags: Put several items that can be identified by feeling, such as a Lego block, a spoon, a toy car, or other small objects, in a fabric bag or large sock. Make one bag for each group of three to six participants.

Super Science FUN! Agenda

First Hour Session

5 minutes | Introduce the topic and then introduce yourself (if working with a group that does not know you).

If planning to conduct the second hour session in addition to the first, pass out the *Check Your Knowledge* sheet to participants and ask them to complete the left-hand side of the sheet. When they finish, ask them to set aside the sheet and not to refer to it until the end of the second session. Tell them that even if they realize that an answer is wrong as they take part in the training, they should not change their answer. This form is to evaluate what they learned in the training and will be anonymous.

13.1

10 minutes | Icebreaker: This icebreaker will stimulate discussion about what is science. Pass out the Icebreaker bags. In small groups, ask participants to share what they can learn from the items in the bag. Help responders think of science concepts that can be learned. Point out how teachers are sometimes not comfortable teaching science, but that there are many opportunities to include science in daily routines. Explain that many common early childhood activities, such as water play and blocks, involve science concepts.

5 minutes | Review the Objectives Part 1. Discuss with the group what they will learn in the session. Ask for specific questions that they want answered during the training.

Objectives Part 1

Set up a developmentally appropriate science center.

Identify the goals of science with young children.

Describe how to integrate science throughout your daily curriculum.

Identify why and how to observe science activities.

Distribute the *Lucky 13 Key Points Science Worksheet* handout. Ask participants to use the sheet for notes to have as a resource for their classrooms.

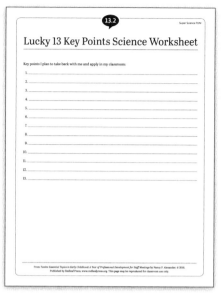

13.2

10 minutes   Distribute the handout *What Is Science?* Use it for discussing and explaining science and its role in the early childhood curriculum. Discuss each concept and how it applies to young children. Point out how children are natural scientists as they explore the world around them. Pass out the *Suggested Science Center Materials* handout. Review the handout and add any additional materials the participants have used.

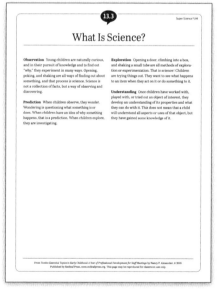

13.3

13.4

Ask participants to name some activities that they do with young children that they consider to be science. Write some of the responses on a flip chart. Some possibilities might be water play, caring for animals or plants, and nature activities.

10 minutes   Reveal and discuss the Science Center Goals flip chart. Review and discuss the goals, and explain that science is not just knowing a collection of facts, but a way of thinking and drawing conclusions based on one's experiences. Science encourages children to question "what if." As teachers, we must strive to make a safe environment for children to explore the world around them and learn from that exploration.

Divide into small groups of three to six. (See tips under "Working with Small Groups and Partners," on page 20.)

10 minutes   Small Group Activity: Pass out the Feely Bags, one bag for each group. Each group member will have an opportunity to reach into the bag and try to determine the items in it within 5 seconds. After everyone has had a turn, ask the groups to discuss what items each person thinks are in the bag. Have them open the bag to see if the group came to a successful conclusion. Ask what more they know about the items—such as color—now that they see them that they could not tell from feeling. Point out the importance of using all the senses to explore items and how children learn from using their senses to explore materials.

Ask participants, "Did you know everything that was in the bag just from those few seconds with it?" Make the point that it takes more than one experience and often the use of more than one sense with an object to understand it.

10 minutes   Brainstorm items that may be put in a science center and how a science center should be set up. Explain how the area should be arranged for children to use independently and include only items children are free to use. Use the "Guidelines for Selecting Science Materials: Teacher Aid," on page 150, as a guide for suggestions. Help participants relate the information to their own work situation. Discuss how one can set up a science center in a classroom and what items can be put in it. Describe how the science center can be set up for children to learn specific concepts. Explain how a science center that is developmentally appropriate will meet children's individual needs and allow for differences in interests and abilities and ways of learning. Use the "Integrating Science into the Curriculum: Teacher Aid," on page 151, as a resource for ideas. Or, a science center can be set up mainly for children to explore the properties of materials.

Review and summarize the content of the session.

Distribute certificates if presenting the one-hour session alone.

Second Hour Session

Have five activities set up in the room and ready to use. See the *Science Activities* handout for ideas for activities. Display an assortment of children's picture books that include science concepts.

Explain to participants that they will explore the science setups just as children would.

13.5

5 minutes   Review the Objectives Part 2. Discuss with the group what they will learn in the session. Ask for specific questions that they want answered during the training.

Objectives Part 2

Participate in science activities appropriate for young children.

Describe the activities and what children learn.

Identify how picture books can be used to develop science concepts.

Define the teacher's role in science.

10 minutes   Discuss the following concepts and give examples: Children approach science naturally and without hesitation. They are not intimidated by the word *science*. They use all their senses to experience items and events, beginning when they are very young. Remind participants that we must keep safety in mind when we set up a science center for young children because they will taste things!

10 minutes   Walkabout Activity: Have participants move around the room to look at and discuss the activities that have been set up. Also, have them review the children's books that include science concepts. Discuss how these books are stories, but they include information that would be considered science concepts. Describe how the books combine science and literacy.

20 minutes
Explain the activities they saw and tell them that now they will experience some age-appropriate science activities firsthand. Discuss the appropriate ages and how the activities can be set up for children to use independently. Distribute the handout *Science Activities*. Have them participate in the activities just as children would. Instruct the participants to move around the room and take part until they have participated in all activities.

10 minutes
Distribute the handout *The Teacher's Role in Science* and discuss the important role of the teacher as a facilitator. Give some examples from your own experience and ask participants to share some of their experiences in how they interact with children. Relate the information to the activities you provided and how you set up the activities for them.

Emphasize the importance of supporting children's construction of knowledge and learning through exploration and discovery.

13.6

5 minutes
Instruct participants to complete the *Check Your Knowledge* forms by answering the questions again and writing their new answers in the blanks on the right-hand side of the paper. Remind them not to change their answers they gave at the beginning of the session. Collect the *Check Your Knowledge* sheets, then hand out certificates and any additional information or materials you wish to provide.

13.1

Alternate, Additional, and Follow-Up Activities

SCIENCE STORY BOOKS

Display children's books that include science concepts, both nonfiction and story-books. Ask participants to review some of the books in small groups and make a list of science concepts included in the books, then report their findings to the whole group.

FIVE SENSES ACTIVITIES

Distribute the handout *Five Senses Activities for Science Centers*, and set up centers for participants to perform the activities as children might do in a science center. Suggest they try the activities themselves before they use them with children.

Ask them to suggest other activities they might use. Point out how children use their senses to explore and learn.

13.7

PROCESS SKILLS IN SCIENCE

Distribute the handout *Process Skills in Science*. Ask participants to identify or create one additional activity for each of the process skills that emphasize the use of that skill.

Emphasize how science education for preschool children is not about learning facts, but about learning the process skills of science.

13.8

PLANNING GUIDE FOR SCIENCE

Distribute the handout *Planning Guide for Science Lesson* for participants to plan a science activity to use in their classroom. Point out that the handouts include things to consider whenever an activity is planned.

Explain how the guide will help them think about the best way to conduct an activity.

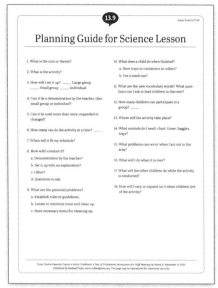

13.9

Resources

CHILDREN'S PICTURE BOOKS WITH SCIENCE CONCEPTS

- ▶ *Autumn Snow: A Unique Leaf Book* by Flitzy Books
- ▶ *Babies of the Wild* by Carl R. Sams II and Jean Stoick
- ▶ *Baby Loves Spring!* by Karen Katz
- ▶ *Dancing in the Rain* by Dee Smith
- ▶ *First the Egg*, by Laura Vaccaro Seeger
- ▶ *Fly High Fly Low* by Don Freeman
- ▶ *Hello, World! Backyard Bugs* by Jill McDonald
- ▶ *Hello, World! Birds* by Jill McDonald
- ▶ *In My Pond* by Sara Gillingham
- ▶ *Kitten's First Full Moon* by Kevin Henkes
- ▶ *Lemonade Stand* by Dee Smith
- ▶ *Little Owl's Night* by Divya Srinivasan
- ▶ *Pumpkin Patch Treasure* by Dee Smith
- ▶ *Snowy Day* by Ezra Jack Keats
- ▶ *The Five Colors of Our Nature Walk* by Latisha Jones

▸ *The House in the Night* by Susan Marie Swanson

▸ *The Mitten* by Jan Brett

▸ *The Year Comes Round: Haiku through the Seasons* by Sid Farrar

▸ *Stranger in the Woods* by Carl R. Sams

▸ *Turtles in My Sandbox* by Jennifer Keats Curtis

▸ *Winter Wonderful* by Dee Smith

ADDITIONAL SCIENCE RESOURCES

▸ Boston Children's Museum. 2013. *STEM Sprouts Teaching Guide*. Boston, MA: Boston Children's Museum.

▸ Charlesworth, Rosalind, and Karen Lind. 2013. *Math and Science for Young Children*, 7th ed. Belmont, CA: Wadsworth.

▸ NAEYC. 2015. *Exploring Math and Science in Preschool*. Washington, DC: NAEYC.

Guidelines for Selecting Science Materials: Teacher Aid

1. Are the materials open ended? Can the items be used in more than one way? For example, water play provides opportunities to explore measuring, floating, and evaporation. Food preparation activities involve many science concepts, such as measuring, the effect of heat, and using senses.

2. Are the materials designed for use by children? In science, children do something to materials to make something else happen. For example, if a substance is to be dissolved, which one will offer the best experience for children, salt, sugar, or pudding mix? How can children answer questions for themselves, such as "What happens when one blows up a balloon? How is sand different when it is wet?"

3. Are materials arranged to encourage communication among children? When appropriate, provide materials to encourage cooperation and conversation. Arrange the materials in categories, such as cups of water in an area of the center, substances to be tested in another, and spoons and dishes in another. Children quickly learn to cooperate and communicate in order to complete an activity.

4. Is there a variety of materials? A wide variety of materials allows children to follow their individual interests and to select and explore according to their personal interests.

5. Do the materials encourage "What if . . ." statements? A sink and float activity invites children to predict what will happen if they try to float various objects, such as a marble, a straw, a toy boat, or a sponge. Such an activity lends itself to finding out what happens.

6. Are the materials appropriate for the children's maturity? Consider not only the age, but also the maturity level of the children. Children at the end of the fourth year will be able to handle activities that they could not at the beginning. Select materials that children can handle safely and efficiently.

7. Do the materials allow for individual differences in ability, interest, working space, and style? After considering floating and sinking, some children will begin to consider size and other characteristics of the available objects. Have objects with a variety of textures and features available.

8. How much teacher direction do the materials require? In giving directions, consider the age of the children. Four- and five-year-olds might listen to recorded directions, but three-year-olds and young fours respond best to personal directions. Rebus directions, such as a picture recipe, may also be appropriate.

9. Do the materials stress process skills? Process skills are the fundamental skills emphasized in science explorations with young children. These skills will often come naturally from manipulating a variety of appropriate materials.

Integrating Science into the Curriculum: Teacher Aid

Opportunities abound for teaching science in early childhood. Actively involve children with art, blocks, dramatic play, language arts, math, and creative movement. Here are a few ideas to begin with:

Painting Fingerpainting helps children learn to perceive with their fingertips and demonstrates the concept of color diffusion as they clean their hands. Shapes can be recognized by painting with familiar objects.

Water or sand center Concepts such as volume and conservation begin to be understood when children measure with water and sand. Buoyancy can be explored with toy boats and sinking and floating objects.

Blocks Blocks are an excellent way to introduce children to friction, gravity, and simple machines.

Books Many books introduce scientific concepts while telling a story. Books with pictures give views of unfamiliar things and an opportunity to explore detail, and infer and discuss.

Music and rhythmic activities Music instruments let children experience the movement of air and vibrations. Air resistance can also be demonstrated by dancing with a scarf.

Playground The playground can provide opportunities to recognize and predict weather, practice balancing, and experience friction.

The concrete world of science integrates especially well with reading and writing. Basic words, object guessing, experience charts, writing stories, and working with tactile sensations all encourage early literacy.

13.10

Brain Development

• The Basics •

Materials for Facilitator

- ▸ Document, Agenda
- ▸ Document, *Check Your Knowledge Answer Key*
- ▸ PowerPoint, Brain Development: The Basics

Materials for Participants

- ▸ *Assessment, Check Your Knowledge*

First Hour

- ▸ Handout, *Neural Connections*
- ▸ Handout, *How You Can Help Babies' Brain Development*
- ▸ Handout, Certificate for Hour One

Second Hour

- ▸ Handout, *Birth to Twelve Months: Areas of Development for Babies*
- ▸ Handout, *Twelve to Twenty-Four Months: What Toddlers Need to Develop*
- ▸ Handout, *Ages Two to Three: Areas of Development for Older Toddlers*
- ▸ Handout, *Six Strategies for Toddler Tantrums*
- ▸ Handout, Certificate for Hour Two

Equipment and Supplies

- ▸ projector and laptop
- ▸ flip charts or poster boards and markers

For First Hour

- ▸ a ball of yarn

For Additional Activities

- ▸ child development charts (See list on page 82 for suggestions.)

Make-Ahead Materials

For First Hour

Key Findings from Brain Research Activity: Print the sheet *Key Findings from Brain Research* and cut the statements into strips.

Fold the strips and put each set in a resealable plastic bag. Make one set for each group of three to six trainees. If each copy is on a different color of paper, the set will be easier to keep organized.

Brain Development: The Basics Agenda

First Hour Session

5 minutes   Introduce the topic and then introduce yourself (if working with a group that does not know you).

If planning to conduct the second hour session in addition to the first, pass out the *Check Your Knowledge* sheet to participants and ask them to complete the left-hand side of the sheet. When they finish, ask them to set aside the sheet and not to refer to it until the end of the second session. Tell them that even if they realize that an answer is wrong as they take part in the training, they should not change their answer. This form is to evaluate what they learned in the training and will be anonymous.

14.1

10 minutes   Icebreaker: Stand in a circle and give one person the ball of yarn. That person introduces herself if the group does not know each other and states one thing she wants to learn in the session. While holding on to the end of the yarn, that person throws the ball to any other person. The second person in turn holds the ball of yarn, makes a similar introduction, and throws the ball while holding on to the yarn. Once everyone has introduced themselves, a spiderweb has been formed with the yarn. If the group is small, go around one more time.

Relate the web to the connections made in babies' brains as they have experiences and interactions. Explain how these connections are pruned if not used.

5 minutes   Review the Objectives Part 1. Discuss with the group what they will learn in the session and how the questions they asked in the icebreaker will be addressed. Ask for any additional questions that they want answered during the training.

Objectives Part 1

Discuss basic information about how neural connections are formed.

Identify key findings from brain research.

Describe ways to interact with babies to support brain development.

5 minutes   Ask participants to use their cell phones and find one fact about infant brain development. Ask a few volunteers to share what they find and tell where they found the information. Write some of the facts they find on a flip chart.

Divide into small groups of three to six. (See tips under "Working with Small Groups and Partners," on page 20.)

10 minutes   Small Group Activity: Distribute the handout *Neural Connections*, and allow time for participants to read the information. Ask participants to share what information they found most enlightening or insightful. Ask them to discuss how the information applies to their work and which of the suggestions they plan to implement. If time permits, ask for a spokesperson to report their favorite ideas to the whole group.

14.2

10 minutes   Small Group Activity: Distribute the resealable plastic bags containing the *Key Findings from Brain Research* strips. Give the following instructions:

Each participant will choose one of the strips. In some cases, participants may choose more than one so that all strips are selected. One at a time, participants will read their strips to their group. The group will then discuss what that statement means to them and how they can apply the information in their work. If time permits, ask a spokesperson to share some of the group's key points in the discussion with the whole group.

14.3

10 minutes   Small Group Activity: Distribute the handout *How You Can Help Babies' Brain Development*. Allow time for participants to read and discuss the information. Ask them to add their own ideas in the space provided. Explain that even if they work with preschoolers or toddlers, knowledge of brain development is important in understanding how the early interactions are important in a child's development. If time permits, ask for a spokesperson from each group to report their favorite ideas to the whole group.

14.4

5 minutes   Review and summarize the content of the session.

Distribute certificates if presenting the one-hour session alone.

Second Hour Session

5 minutes   Review the Objectives Part 2. Discuss with the group what they will learn in the session. Ask for specific questions that they want answered during the training.

> ### Objectives Part 2
>
> Identify ways to support brain development related to the ages of children.
>
> Apply information about brain development to the work setting.

Divide into small groups of three to six. (See tips under "Working with Small Groups and Partners," on page 20.)

15 minutes — Small Group Activity: Distribute the handout *Birth to Twelve Months: Areas of Development for Babies*. Ask each group to review the handout and discuss the ways to support development. Ask each group to agree on some additional ways to support brain development and write them in the space provided. Have each group select a spokesperson to share the group's suggestions with the whole group.

Ask for ideas of how they might communicate this information to families, especially those who have infants.

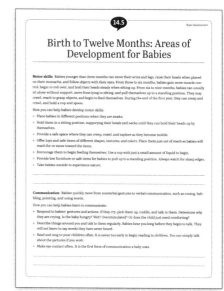

14.5

10 minutes — Small Group Activity: Distribute the handout *Twelve to Twenty-Four Months: What Toddlers Need to Develop*. Ask each group to review the handout and discuss ways to support development. Ask each group to agree on some additional ways to support brain development and write them in the space provided. Have each group select a spokesperson to share the group's suggestions with the whole group.

If time permits, ask for additional ways to communicate this information to families.

14.6

10 minutes   Distribute the handout *Ages Two to Three: Areas of Development for Older Toddlers.* Ask each group to review the handout and discuss ways to support development at this age. Ask each group to agree on some additional ways to support brain development and write them in the space provided. Have each group select a spokesperson to share the group's suggestions with the whole group.

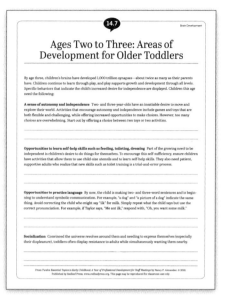

14.7

Have each person select a partner. (See tips under "Working with Small Groups and Partners," on pages 20–23.)

15 minutes   Partner Activity: Review the information on the handout *Focus on Brain Development from 3–5 Years.* After reading the handout, complete the charts at the bottom. Instruct partners to work together to plan how they will support brain development in the four domains. Then have them list in the appropriate box how they will address the 5 principles.

14.8

5 minutes   Instruct participants to complete the *Check Your Knowledge* forms by answering the questions again and writing their new answers in the blanks on the right-hand side of the paper. Remind them not to change their answers they gave at the beginning of the session. Collect the *Check Your Knowledge* sheets, then hand out certificates and any additional information or materials you wish to provide.

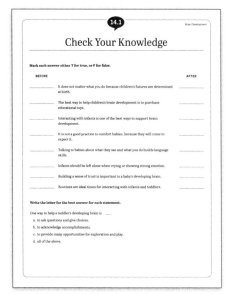

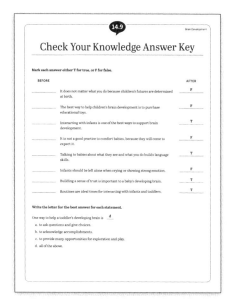

14.1   14.9

Alternate, Additional, and Follow-Up Activities

FINE- AND GROSS-MOTOR SKILLS

Give each participant a copy of the following paragraph or write it on a flip chart. Ask them to think of all the motor skills mastered by toddlers. If they have difficulty, pass around some development charts for ideas.

Toddlers have a wide range of fine- and gross-motor skills. They can scribble with crayons, roll playdough, turn pages in a book, tear collage materials, and fingerpaint. They are comfortable walking and running, hopping and climbing. They roll, throw, and catch balls. Encourage toddlers to try new skills, and support their efforts for continued motor development.

PLAY EQUALS LEARNING

Give each participant a copy of the following list or write it on a flip chart. Ask them to think of as many things as they can that children learn through play. Ask them to write their ideas on a flip chart.

> Children are learning constantly from the moment they are born.
>
> This most important learning comes from play.
>
> When a baby plays with blocks, she is learning about shapes and colors, and developing fine-motor coordination.
>
> When a toddler spills milk on the floor, he is learning science, gravity, and sound. When he creates a pretend story with stuffed animals, he is learning to create and carry out a plan.
>
> Play is also a way children learn to understand feelings.
>
> When children are free to follow their own ideas, they have many learning opportunities.

FOLLOW INFANTS' AND TODDLERS' LEAD

Ask participants in small groups to use the following scenario as a basis for a role play. Ask each small group to create a role play scenario that is appropriate for the ages with which they work and that demonstrates good interactions. Then have the groups demonstrate how to respond.

As you play with a baby or toddler, talk to her about what you are doing, and show her things. Let the child take the lead at times. Observe, and then base your response or action on what seems to interest her.

> A caregiver, Maria, holding an infant, David, notices that he seems to be looking at the mobile hanging over a crib. Maria says, "Oh, do you see that?" and takes David over to touch it. Later, when playing with blocks, Maria builds a small tower, and David happily knocks it down. Maria waits to see what David will do next. He picks up a block and holds it out to Maria, who takes it and says, "What do you want to do with this green block?" and offers it back. David takes it and places it on the floor, then picks up another block and holds it out. Maria takes it and puts it on top of the green block. Then Maria picks up a red block and holds it out.

Babies and toddlers love this type of back and forth activity. It prepares them to take initiative in their own learning. When you follow a child's lead, you're giving her practice at taking those steps while providing support.

References and Resources

Alexander, Nancy. 2012. *Nailing Jelly to the Wall: Defining and Providing Technical Assistance in Early Childhood Education*. Lewisville, NC: Gryphon House.

———. 2000. *Early Childhood Workshops That Work!: The Essential Guide to Successful Training and Workshops*. Beltsville, MD: Gryphon House.

Banning, Wendy, and Ginny Sullivan. 2011. *Lens on Outdoor Learning*. St. Paul, MN: Redleaf Press.

Bilmes, Jenna. 2004. *Beyond Behavior Management: The Six Life Skills Children Need to Thrive in Today's World*. St. Paul, MN: Redleaf Press.

Boston Children's Museum. *STEM Sprouts Teaching Guide*. Accessed January 2017. http://www.bostonchildrensmuseum.org/sites/default/files/pdfs/STEMGuide .pdf.

Burman, Lisa. 2009. *Are You Listening?: Fostering Conversations That Help Young Children Learn*. St. Paul, MN: Redleaf Press.

Charlesworth, Rosalind, and Karen K. Lind. 2013. *Math and Science for Young Children*. 7th ed. Belmont, CA: Wadsworth.

Curtis, Deb, and Margie Carter. 2000. *The Art of Awareness: How Observation Can Transform Your Teaching*. St. Paul, MN: Redleaf Press.

Daly, Lisa, and Miriam Beloglovsky. 2015. *Loose Parts: Inspiring Play in Young Children*. St. Paul, MN: Redleaf Press.

Darling-Kuria, Nikki. 2010. *Brain-Based Early Learning Activities: Connecting Theory and Practice*. St. Paul, MN: Redleaf Press.

Dombro, Amy Laura, Judy Jablon, and Charlotte Stetson. 2011. *Powerful Interactions: How to Connect with Children to Extend Their Learning*. Washington, DC: NAEYC.

Donohue, Chip. 2017. *Family Engagement in the Digital Age: Early Childhood Educators as Media Mentors*. New York: Routledge.

Duncan, Sandra, Jody Martin, and Rebecca Kreth. 2016. *Rethinking the Classroom Landscape: Creating Environments That Connect Young Children, Families, and Communities*. Lewisville, NC: Gryphon House.

Ernst, Johanna Darragh. 2014. *The Welcoming Classroom: Building Strong Home-to-School Connections for Early Learning*. Lewisville, NC: Gryphon House.

Feeney, Stephanie, Nancy K. Freeman, and Eva Moravcik. 2016. *Teaching the NAEYC Code of Ethical Conduct: A Resource Guide*. Rev. ed. Washington, DC: NAEYC.

Fennimore, Beatrice Schneller. 2014. *Standing Up for Something Every Day: Ethics and Justice in Early Childhood Classrooms*. New York: Teachers College Press.

Forrester, Michelle, and Kay M. Albrecht. 2009. *SET for Life: Social Emotional Tools for Life*. Houston:

Innovations in Early Childhood. Gronlund, Gaye. 2010. *Developmentally Appropriate Play: Guiding Young Children to a Higher Level*. St. Paul, MN: Redleaf Press.

Gronlund, Gaye, and Marlyn James. 2005. *Focused Observations: How to Observe Children for Assessment and Curriculum Planning*. St. Paul, MN: Redleaf Press.

Heroman, Cate. 2016. *Making and Tinkering with STEM: Solving Design Challenges with Young Children*. Washington, DC: NAEYC.

HighScope Research Foundation. 2017. "For Parents." Retrieved March 20, 2017. https://highscope.org/families/parents.

Hoffman, John. 2009. "Early Brain Development." *Today's Parent*. October 5. Accessed January 2017. http://www.todaysparent.com/baby/baby-health/early-brain-development/.

Honig, Alice S. 1996. *Love and Learn: Positive Guidance for Young Children*. Washington, DC: NAEYC.

Isbell, Rebecca, and Betty Exelby. 2001. *Early Learning Environments That Work!* Beltsville, MD: Gryphon House.

Jablon, Judy, Amy Laura Dembro, and Shaun Johnson. 2014. *Coaching with Powerful Interactions: A Guide for Partnering with Early Childhood Teachers*. Washington, DC: NAEYC.

Keeler, Rusty. 2016. *Seasons of Play: Natural Environments of Wonder*. Lewisville, NC: Gryphon House.

Keyser, Janis. 2006. *From Parents to Partners: Building a Family-Centered Early Childhood Program*. St. Paul, MN: Redleaf Press.

Kohl, MaryAnn F. 1999. *Making Make-Believe: Fun Props, Costumes, and Creative Play Ideas*. Beltsville, MD: Gryphon House.

Lerner, Claire, and Rebecca Parlakian. 2007. *Learning Happens: 30 Video Vignettes of Babies and Toddlers Learning School Readiness Skills*. DVD. Washington, DC: Zero to Three.

McCracken, Janet Brown. 1987. *Play Is FUNdamental*. Washington, DC: NAEYC.

McNelis, Deborah. 2010. *Naturally Developing Young Brains: Supporting Brain Development for 3–5-Year-Olds through Natural Environments*. Milwaukee, WI: Brain Insights.

NAEYC (National Association for the Education of Young Children). 2012. *Technology and Interactive Media as Tools in Early Childhood Programs Serving Children from Birth through Age 8*. http://www.naeyc.org/files/naeyc/file/positions/PS_technology_WEB2.pdf.

———. 2011. *Code of Ethical Conduct and Statement of Commitment*. Washington, DC: NAEYC.

———. 2009. *Where We Stand on responding to linguistic and cultural diversity*. https://www.naeyc.org/files/naeyc/file/positions/diversity.pdf.

———. 1995. *Responding to Linguistic and Cultural Diversity: Recommendations for Effective Early Childhood Education.* https://www.naeyc.org/files/naeyc/file /positions/PSDIV98.PDF.

Nelson, Eric. 2012. *Cultivating Outdoor Classrooms: Designing and Implementing Child-Centered Learning Environments.* St. Paul, MN: Redleaf Press.

NSTA (National Science Teachers Association). 2014. *Early Childhood Science Education.* Washington, DC: NAEYC.

Plaster, Liz, and Rick Krustchinsky. 2010. *Incredible Edible Science: Recipes for Developing Science and Literacy Skills.* St. Paul, MN: Redleaf Press.

Powers, Julie. 2016. *Parent Engagement in Early Learning: Strategies for Working with Families.* St. Paul, MN: Redleaf Press.

Simon, Fran, and Karen Nemeth. 2012. *Digital Decisions: Choosing the Right Technology Tools for Early Childhood Education.* Lewisville, NC: Gryphon House.

Zero to Three. "Brain Development." Accessed January 2017. https://www.zerotothree .org/early-learning/brain-development.

Certificate
of Achievement

This certificate is presented to

_____

for completing a **1-hour session** of the professional development program:

Twelve Essential Topics in Early Childhood:

_____
[name of session]

Nancy P. Alexander
Nancy P. Alexander

_____
[date]

Redleaf Press®
www.redleafpress.org
800-423-8309

Certificate
of Achievement

This certificate is presented to

_____

for completing a **1-hour session** of the professional development program:

Twelve Essential Topics in Early Childhood:

_____
[name of session]

Redleaf Press®
www.redleafpress.org
800-423-8309

_____
[date]

The author and Redleaf Press have not verified the actual completion of the program by this participant.

Certificate
of Achievement

This certificate is presented to

_____

for completing a **2-hour session** of the professional development program:

Twelve Essential Topics in Early Childhood:

_____

[name of session]

_____

Nancy P. Alexander
Nancy P. Alexander

Redleaf Press®
www.redleafpress.org
800-423-8309

_____
[date]

Certificate of Achievement

This certificate is presented to

_____

for completing a **2-hour session** of the professional development program:

Twelve Essential Topics in Early Childhood:

_____
[name of session]

_____
[date]

Redleaf Press®
www.redleafpress.org
800-423-8309

The author and Redleaf Press have not verified the actual completion of the program by this participant.